MANAGING PUBLIC SERVICES INNOVATION

The experience of English housing associations

Richard M. Walker, Emma L. Jeanes and
Robert O. Rowlands

The POLICY
P ~ P
PRESS

First published in Great Britain in April 2001 by

The Policy Press
University of Bristol
34 Tyndall's Park Road
Bristol BS8 1PY
UK

Tel +44 (0)117 954 6800
Fax +44 (0)117 973 7308
E-mail tpp@bristol.ac.uk
www.policypress.org.uk

ISBN 1 86134 294 2

Dr Richard M. Walker is a Senior Lecturer in the Department of City and Regional Planning at Cardiff University. **Dr Emma L. Jeanes** is a Lecturer in the School of Business and Economics at Exeter University. **Robert O. Rowlands** is a Research Assistant in the Centre for Housing Management and Development at Cardiff University.

Cover design by Qube Design Associates, Bristol

Printed in Great Britain by Hobbs the Printers Ltd, Southampton

Contents

List of tables, figures and boxes

Tables

Figures

Boxes

Acknowledgements

The research reported on in this book was funded by the Economic and Social Research Council (ESRC) on the Innovation Programme (L125251057) and The Housing Corporation. East Dorset, Riverside and Touchstone Housing Associations gave their time freely to the research and supported stage two. The views expressed here are those of the authors alone.

The steering group for the ESRC-funded element provided useful and critical commentary on the research as it progressed. Thanks are expressed to Dr Fiona Steele, the Director of the ESRC's Innovation Programme, who chaired the steering group and provided support throughout the research programme. Professor Richard Whipp of Cardiff Business School, together with Helen Norey and Glyn Taylor, are also thanked. The key contacts from our collaborative housing associations also sat on this group and need special mention. Caroline Field from Riverside, Graeme Stanley from East Dorset (and now at Weymouth and Portland Housing) and Andrew Thomas from Touchstone (now at Ridge) all gave their time freely and gave us access to their organisations. Without them and the several hundred people that we interviewed the research reported in this book would not have been possible.

As with all acknowledgements there are too many names and too little space. The housing associations that gave us access to stage two of the project are thanked. These are: The Amphion Partnership (Amicus, Hyde, Hastoe), Black Country, Bradford and Northern, Guinness Trust Home, Irwell Valley, Knightstone, North British, Thames Valley. In addition many people at conferences and in our respective universities have listened to our ideas and work with interest and provided us with useful feedback. We would like to mention George Boyne, Bob Smith, Karen Dickens and Isabel Sawyer at Cardiff University and David Pickernell at Exeter.

Summary

Innovation is now expected of public services organisations with the aim of improving their performance and increasing the quality of services. These expectations extend beyond the shores of Britain and are not just the prerogative of the Labour government and its 'modernisation' agenda. They are international, described in the USA as 'Reinventing Government' and clearly seen in the English-speaking nations of the world. However, the innovative capacity of public services organisations is not widely proven. Furthermore, if public services organisations are to meet their innovative expectations, as exhorted to by government, precious little information exists on the management of innovation to help in this pursuit. This study explores the innovative claims of one group of public services organisations: housing associations or Registered Social Landlords. They are excellent examples to draw upon. They were propelled into the centre stage of housing policy in the late 1980s because they were seen to be innovative. Extensive change has subsequently taken place within the sector and they have increasingly experienced exposure to the market, beyond that encountered in many other public services organisations. Our findings have relevance to the housing association sector and to other public services organisations that are facing similar experiences as the market comes to play an increasingly important role in our hospitals, local authorities and universities. Our work reports on:

- the policy context which makes innovation imperative;
- the nature of housing association innovation;
- the characteristics of innovative housing associations;
- the management of innovation, with recommendations for best practice; and
- proposals on techniques for sharing innovation knowledge and best practice within the sector.

The findings from this work are important as public policies become more 'evidence-based'. The evidence presented in the book, from which our lessons are drawn, is based on longitudinal case studies of housing associations and data sets, including the Housing Corporation's

Innovation and Good Practice database on housing association innovation. The research was undertaken between 1997 and 2000.

Innovation

The notion of innovation came into popular use within the housing association sector during the 1990s as government and national housing agencies started to promote the importance of innovation and associations themselves claimed to be innovative. However, housing associations' claims to their innovative capacity are unproven and because guidance from government on innovation is limited, it was appropriate to research the nature, extent and scope of innovation among housing associations.

Innovation is a highly complex concept (Chapter 2). It is not therefore possible to offer a discrete definition. Rather a range of dimensions of the concept can be drawn out. Innovation is:

- a process, through which new ideas, objects and practices are created, developed or reinvented;
- related to the introduction and application of ideas within a role, group or organisation;
- most commonly associated with processes, products or procedures, or outcomes;
- something new and novel to the relevant unit of adoption (that is a person, organisation or sector), rather than newness per se;
- designed with the intent of benefiting the individual, the group, organisation or wider society, though an innovation may have a negative and unanticipated impact;
- finally, and importantly, it is associated with discontinuous change, 'framebreaking' rather than 'framebending', and a process of creative destruction.

The complexity of the concept of innovation is reflected in the literature. Innovation research is a rich and extensive field with thousands of articles published. Our work focuses upon two themes within the field. Organisational innovativeness research seeks to discover the determinants of an organisation's propensity to innovate and focuses upon organisational characteristics. Our second stream is the management of innovation which is concerned with how innovation is managed, and how an organisation moves from an idea to a finished product or service.

Innovation drivers

It is now beyond doubt that the need for innovation is essential (Chapters 3 and 6). A range of internal and external pressures are leading to innovation:

- Government agendas are increasingly dynamic in housing and public services management. They make it clear that innovation is now expected, while others talk about the need for the social housing sector to be 'reinvented' and to foster a climate of innovation.
- The expectations of the public are changing: no longer do new tenants flock to the doors of the housing office in search of accommodation; the housing officer now needs to search for them!
- The competition for resources and the welfare problems of tenants have led housing associations to diversify their activity away from core social housing business.
- The sector, having being transformed over the last decade by stock transfers is set to be changed beyond recognition as they continue apace.
- Running alongside these housing policy reforms the Social Exclusion Unit has been making recommendations to bring housing to the centre of neighbourhood renewal, reshaping the nature of housing management services and the role of landlords.
- If these reforms were not sufficient, a new regulatory regime has been developed which redefines social housing and sets in place new requirements on associations, alongside the economic regulation of associations.
- Our case-study associations themselves are responding to environmental change and innovating in an attempt to remain 'ahead of the game'.
- They are seeking to improve performance and service quality, and reduce costs while challenging the way things are done.
- Our case-studies were also driving innovation themselves by taking opportunities to develop leadership skills at many levels in the organisation, to see how things are done elsewhere and thereby bring new ideas to the organisation.

Associations have not been idle, some have been willing to take risks and visionary leaders have had the charisma to champion their ideas and get them adopted.

The nature of housing association innovations

As change and turbulence in the environment becomes endemic, innovation has been seen as the antidote, giving associations confidence and a new lease of life (Chapter 4). While government and housing associations themselves have implicitly assumed that independent non-profit housing organisations were innovative and able to meet new challenges, we have provided the first empirical evidence to support this case. The evidence indicates that housing associations do have innovative capacity and are capable of 'framebreaking' activities rather than just 'framebending'. Our databases have identified innovation in nearly twenty per cent of all housing associations and proportions of 'total' innovations similar to those found in the private and voluntary sectors in other research.

Our two-stage innovation classification system describes these innovations. This allows us to make broad generalisations from the findings and provides information to practitioners about the management implications of the innovations they are adopting. Stage one examines whether an innovation involves new or existing services, which are delivered to new or existing users. This leads to four types of innovation:

A typology of housing association innovation with examples

Innovation type	Definition	Example
Total	Providing new services to new users	Diversification (eg private renting, housing plus) and customer focus (eg call centres)
Evolutionary	Providing new services to exisiting customers	Organisational structures (eg new organisational structures)
Expansionary	Providing services to new users	Organisational expansion (eg stock transfers, mergers)
Development or incremental	Modifying services and provision which have supported innovations	New management techniques such as TQM or BPR and cultural change programmes

The second aspect was the detailed nature of each innovation which the classification system looked at to identify its attributes, which include organisational focus, radicalness, centrality, adaptability, uncertainty, pervasiveness and risk.

This level of detail about the nature of innovation is important for managing innovation. Total innovations will require new skills and management approaches and may raise challenges to other public services institutions, such as the industry regulator.

The innovative housing association

Housing associations have developed a range of innovations but what are the characteristics of these innovative housing associations? If these are known it will be possible for associations to emulate them, to rank and compare themselves against our population of innovative associations, and the archetypal innovative association. The explanations of the innovative housing association we offer relate to the people or actors in associations, the nature of the organisation and its management. Working from our databases we have found that innovation is more likely to be found in some associations than in others (Chapter 5). The 'typical' innovative housing association has been shown to have the following characteristics:

- it will be a larger association with 6,000 homes, if not more;
- it will have specialist staff, with support and development staff being particularly important, whereas a large number of housing management staff will reduce the capacity for innovation;
- it will have a high proportion of professional staff;
- it will work in nearly thirty different local authorities, if not more;
- it will have a variety of tasks and functions bringing together different skills and departments.

The innovative housing association fits the picture of a 'regional' association. This is a significant finding given the likely transfer of swathes of local government housing stock into the association sector over the next decade. The government has suggested that the maximum size of a transfer association should be 12,000 homes. This ceiling, which many organisations are likely to approach, would suggest that innovation will continue apace in the sector – size is an important characteristic. However, transfer organisations are unlikely to score on the range of variables that characterise the innovative association. For example, they will be geographically restricted, initially, to one locality, or part thereof. Furthermore, the process of adaptation and change following transfer is a long and slow one. We could therefore see innovation decrease in proportionate and absolute terms, as the nature of the sector is transformed.

The existence of a large development team is an important innovative characteristic. This partly supports the rhetoric of housing associations during the 1990s when they argued that associations had to 'develop or die'. However, given the changing nature of the development process, which has moved away from greenfield new build to regeneration, it is possible to hypothesise that substantial regeneration activity at an association could bring the same dynamic process. However, the critical difference here that a development team has from a regeneration team is the expansionary activities.

These findings lead to the conclusion that the innovative association might not fit the ideal type of organisation that is alluded to in government publications. It might be neither regeneration-focused, nor housing management-focused nor tenant-focused but more managerial in its composition. Small housing organisations, with less than 1,000 homes, are more conducive to good organisational performance and high levels of tenant involvement. This implies that the policy objectives laid down by government may be mutually incompatible – innovation equals big, tenant-friendly equals small.

Managing innovation in housing associations

An important area of enquiry was concerned with the way in which innovation is managed. Growing evidence has been presented elsewhere to indicate that the management of innovation is not a simple and straightforward process of developing ideas, gaining support for them, adopting and implementing them and ensuring that they become routine (Chapter 2). Rather there are key events which overlap, while the stages in the process of managing innovation come backwards and forwards. Three key phases are nonetheless observed:

(1) initiation
(2) development, and
(3) implementation or termination.

Given that the management of innovation is iterative then it is not a smooth journey of regular staging posts and clear signposts (Chapters 2 and 6). Rather, innovation is a journey through uncharted waters that will lead organisations down stray tributaries which become un-navigable and through the rush of rapids that leads the initiation, development and implementation of innovation. Clear lessons for the successful management of innovation to emerge from this study include:

- Boundary-scanning activities provide an important store of knowledge that aids future innovation initiation and development by looking outside the sector and bringing ideas back to it.
- Leaders need to be willing to challenge the status quo and consider new ways of doing things to be ahead of the game.
- Innovation capacity is greater where associations proactively interact with their environment, in addition to understanding the environment from their own perspective. However, looking outside is not the function of leaders alone.
- The process of securing resources for innovation projects often leads the innovation champion to overstate the likely performance achievements of the project to gain support from decision makers.
- Innovations will proliferate into various projects as they are developed. This is to be expected as ideas flow from the original concept. Bundles or families of innovations are useful ways to ensure that a final innovation is delivered as setbacks frequently occur on the innovation journey. Alternative and complementary innovations are one way to ensure forward movement in the search for continuous improvement.
- Interdisciplinary project teams are essential for successful innovation development and implementation. They allow a range of skills, competencies and attitudes to be brought together to match the need of the project. Teams also facilitate innovation implementation by 'spreading the word' and demonstrating how the new and old can be combined to move forward.
- Experiments, demonstration projects and selective implementation can be used to flesh out innovation ideas and work up projects into clear policies and procedures for implementation across the wider organisation, providing the innovation team and others within the association with evidence of what works. This 'deep' development and implementation of innovation resulted in the successful diffusion of innovations within our case-study associations, but is contingent upon top management's continued sponsorship and championing of innovation projects. It also allowed others to anticipate the arrival of

new ways of working and explore, within their own setting, the likely impact of the innovation.

- Partnership innovations will be more complex to manage than internal innovations and associations should expect more setbacks, a higher level of conflict and changing personnel all of which can elongate project time scales.
- Full implementation of innovations will be enhanced by management practices that reinforce the desired innovation behaviour in staff. Performance systems that identify clearly to staff the desired behaviour are successful in achieving this, whether they be directly linked to pay or to appraisal systems. These help to overcome the difficult process of unlearning old practices and bringing about new ways of behaving.

Tracking housing association innovation for best practice

Approaches to the longitudinal study of innovation have been adopted which should help evidence-based policies to be developed. First, we have provided a baseline of innovative activity in the housing association sector through our adoption of the Literature-Based Innovation Output Indicator (Chapter 4). This technique, which relies upon reported innovations and uses bibliographic approaches, has shown that associations have primarily developed evolutionary and incremental innovation, with limited examples of total and expansionary innovations (see table on p x). Databases such as this provide government and its agencies with the opportunity to establish longitudinal studies that will mean that:

- innovation can be tracked over time to understand the nature of the innovations being developed;
- the changing innovativeness of a sector can be monitored and compared with other public services sectors;
- the relationship between innovation and performance can be explored to develop cutting-edge best practice.

These techniques can be developed without burdening organisations through questionnaire surveys and are therefore easy to maintain. They also allow best practice to be easily identified for public services organisations and their decision makers and make evidence widely available. It is now for government to make something of these techniques.

Second, we have researched the management of innovation through time, adopting the longitudinal, comparative and processual case-study methodology from the change research literature. This approach unlocked key questions: first the 'what' of innovation or its content – here associations told us what their innovations were without the research team imposing ideas of what an innovation was; second, the 'why' of innovation or its context; and third, the 'how' of innovation or its processes and management. This involved tracking innovations through 'real time' and retrospectively at each of our case-study associations. Innovation stories were collected from different people in the organisational hierarchy and the results contrasted. This was supplemented by attending meetings, examining internal documentation and researching partner organisations. This detailed examination and comparison between different associations has allowed us to draw the practical conclusions on the management of innovation reported in Chapter 6. It brings attention to the way in which detailed knowledge has to be collected in order to provide useful evidence.

Innovation and regulation

The Blair government has provided continuity in management reforms with the previous Conservative administration by expanding the regulation of public services with, for example, the Best Value Inspectorate in local government. Innovation and regulation are simultaneously concerned with change: innovation with discontinuous change and regulation with effecting change to achieve predetermined standards. Housing associations have been challenging the framework of predetermined standards set for them. Indeed they have been smashing through their 'regulatory net'. Through this study we have seen the regulator legitimising housing association innovation – housing associations have been challenging regulatory boundaries to achieve discontinuity and the Housing Corporation has brought these innovations into its net through its regulatory instruments, a revised regulatory regime and its sponsorship of innovation.

What makes the regulation of the innovations discussed here complex is the dynamic nature of the innovation process. Therefore, it is difficult for the regulator to set standards and monitor new developments because uncertainty exists about them, standards of behaviour have not been established and no monitoring data exists to be collected on their performance. The promotion of innovation and good practice by the regulator attempts to capture this discontinuity and challenges to its framework while sending clear signals to associations about the forms of behaviour expected of them. Standard setting and the effecting of change are therefore controlled to reflect what the regulator sees as the key issues and provides a climate for innovation within boundaries. Current attempts by the regulator to limit the proportion of activity that is non-core or innovatory are a direct result of these difficulties.

It will remain necessary to have a strong regulatory regime to monitor and scrutinise associations because associations have been innovating and framebreaking for a number of years. It is likely that change to the regulatory regime to capture this activity will not stop associations innovating or the regulator developing new innovative policies. In particular, associations have the capacity to innovate, they have ongoing problems to resolve, and therefore innovation will continue apace. This model of regulation increasingly reflects that of the privatised utilities. As housing associations have become more private in their attitudes and outlook, though still remaining public services organisations because of the high levels of subsidy currently and historically invested in them, so the industry regulator has moved into the area of economic regulation. This is squeezing costs while expecting innovation by associations in response. It is a delicate line between enhancing innovation and constraining it.

The clear lesson to housing associations is that if they want to be innovative they need to challenge the boundaries of their activities to deliver the innovations that they have been identifying over the last decade as necessary to deal with their changing external environment. This will include scanning the environment for new opportunities while understanding the attributes of innovations and the management skills needed for adoption and implementation. This relationship between the regulator and housing associations can therefore provide a framework that allows for successful innovation because associations try to break the mould. Consequently we propose that organisations will innovate in highly regulated sectors by 'challenging the boundaries' but that regulator restriction of the scope of organisational activity could eventually reduce innovation and damage the chance of achieving the Best Value management aims of continuous improvement and innovation itself – the regulator and associations need to work together to ensure that this does not happen.

ONE

Introduction

Public services organisations are now expected to innovate in their delivery of services. This is an international expectation clearly linked to the range of management reforms which swept across the world during the last two decades (Pollitt and Bouckaert, 2000). They are currently seen in the development of the 'Reinventing Government' movement in the USA (Osborne and Gaebler, 1992) and the British Labour government's 'Modernisation' agenda (DETR, 1998). These expectations have led to innovative claims by public services organisations. These claims remain unproven. Furthermore, if public services organisations are to meet their innovative expectations little information exists on the management of innovation to help in this pursuit.

This book explores the innovative claims of one group of public services organisations – housing associations (or Registered Social Landlords, as they have been called since the 1996 Housing Act)[1]. It builds upon other innovation case studies (Osborne, 1998; Newman et al, 2000). It offers an alternative perspective by focusing upon and making recommendations on the management of innovation. Housing associations or Registered Social Landlords (we choose to refer to them as housing associations) are particularly good examples to draw upon. They were propelled into the centre stage of housing policy in the late 1980s because they were seen to be innovative. Since this time widespread change has taken place within the sector and housing associations have experienced exposure to the market in more extensive ways than many other public services organisations. However, because other public services organisations will face similar experiences over coming years with the market coming to play an increasingly important role in our hospitals, local authorities and universities, and policy becoming 'evidence-based' as 'what works is what counts' becomes the rhetoric of the day, the findings presented here have relevance in these other settings. The evidence presented in the book, from which our lessons are drawn, is based on extensive and intensive research projects on housing association innovation.

The notion of innovation came into popular use during the 1990s within the housing association sector.

- Key bodies in the housing sector promote the importance of innovation. For example, the Chartered Institute of Housing's Annual Innovation Awards and the Housing Corporation's Innovation and Good Practice Grants.
- The term has been adopted by and used in housing associations on a regular basis, for example housing association self-description, promotional material and branding variously describing themselves as 'innovative and progressive' (Leicester), 'developing innovative ideas' (London and Quadrant), 'renowned for our innovative, analytical approach to housing and homelessness problems' (Notting Hill) and 'developing new and innovative ways' (Riverside). Thus associations feel confident enough to describe themselves as innovative organisations.
- At organisational level, the concept of innovation is captured through the behaviour of associations. This is associated with the notion of 'diversification', as associations move into new areas of provision and service delivery (Clapham and Evans, 1998; Mullins, 1997a).

Housing association innovation, however, remains equivocal. One factor that intuitively leads to questions about the possibility of innovation in housing associations is the nature and level of the industry regulator's control over them. Research in other parts of Britain has shown that housing associations are some of the most extensively regulated public services organisations (Ashworth et al, 1999) as they are subjected to inspection, audit, performance indicators, plans and financial and budgetary controls. Regulation would appear to be the anathema of innovation. It conjures up images of mechanistic behaviour associated with bureaucratic and inflexible ways of working and control systems and processes, whereas innovation is an organic and emergent concept (Burns and Stalker, 1962). Conversely the role of the regulator, in a sector where market forces are historically weak, is to encourage innovation through whatever means are possible – for example the innovation and good practice framework referred to above, which aims to operate as an innovative diffusion system. The interaction between these two areas will form an important part of our analysis in this book.

The need, expectation or requirement for public services organisations, and housing associations in particular, to innovate have their origins in the late 1980s and 1990s. Yet the expectation and exhortation for associations to innovate is still with us:

- The Institute for Public Policy Research's report *Housing United* (2000) talks about the need for the social housing sector to be 'reinvented' and to foster a climate of innovation.
- Government proposals (DETR, 2000) are set to transform the provision of social housing; with housing associations projected to be the only providers of social housing in the medium term, greater emphasis will be placed on strategic housing issues while pressures will be brought on rents.
- Running alongside these housing policy reforms the Social Exclusion Unit (SEU, 2000) has been making recommendations to bring housing to the centre of neighbourhood renewal, reshaping the nature of housing management services and the role of landlords.
- In addition to these reforms a new regulatory regime has been developed (Housing Corporation, 1999). This has redefined social housing as:

> homes for letting or low-cost homeownership and associated amenities and services for people whose personal circumstances make it difficult for them to meet their housing needs in the open market. [It] ... covers schemes for workers in key public services; PFI schemes involving ownership and management; community regeneration initiatives; residential care homes and low-cost homeownership schemes. The definition excludes market-rented schemes, student accommodation and some registered nursing homes. (Dow, 2000, pp 12-13)

It also controls diversity, through financial measures, and will define an association with more than 5% of its turnover or capital in non-core activities as a diversified organisation. A diversified association is subjected to an escalator of regulatory intervention rising in intensity as diversification intensifies.

The need for associations to manage innovation has never been so critical, and will remain so for many years to come as these factors play themselves out and new pressures are brought to bear.

Though the findings reported here will be contingent upon the experience of housing associations, the range of reforms across many of our public services means that these lessons and experiences have wider validity. For example regulatory regimes have been established and are being put into practice across all local government services and the NHS and they will need to learn to manage these two contradictory forces. One of the most important influences on organisational behaviour in the housing association sector has been private finance. Individual housing associations have been working with this for nearly two decades and the sector as a whole for the last ten years. Other public services organisations are beginning to experience similar pressures through, for example, the Private Finance Initiative and the pressures to raise resources outside the public sector, as seen in the debate on the future funding of higher education.

Through this book the authors demonstrate that housing associations have innovative capacity, that innovation is more likely to be found in particular types of housing association and that there are key organisational and managerial characteristics of the innovative housing association. The management of innovation, based upon our study of the innovation process, is shown to be a journey of complexity and uncertainty. In addition to reporting new empirical evidence, the book will draw out a range of useful lessons on the management of innovation which should aid housing associations and other public services organisations in their quest to manage the challenge of innovation.

Aims and objectives

We have noted that innovation is at the heart of government policy. From the Cabinet Office down to the day-to-day management of public services organisations innovation is expected (see for example, Cabinet Office, 2000; DETR, 1998). The Social Exclusion Unit (SEU, 2000, p 24) talks about the "need to use innovation ... to crack persistent, complex problems". However, given that the claims by public services organisations of their innovative capacity are unproven and that guidance from government on the management of innovation (that is the initiation, development and implementation of innovation) is limited, it leaves little knowledge and evidence about the nature, extent and scope of innovation in the public services. This book addresses these omissions through our discussion of five aspects of housing association innovation. It:

- explains the policy context which makes innovation imperative,
- classifies innovation,
- explores the characteristics of innovative organisations,
- examines the management of innovation, and

- develops techniques for sharing innovation knowledge and best practice within the sector.

By focusing upon the lessons from our new empirical research together with theory and evidence from other sectors, the book will help managers in the housing association sector and other public services sectors in their quest for innovation. This book fills an important gap in research on the management of innovation in public services.

Research strategy

The research reported by the authors was undertaken between the summers of 1997 and 2000. The project was conducted in two stages. Stage one was an in-depth, inductive study to ascertain the nature and extent of innovation in housing associations and the processes they used to manage innovation. This work was undertaken in three housing associations. Stage two took these findings to the wider association sector. Bibliographic sources were used to classify innovations across the sector, the characteristics of these innovative organisations were explored and the findings generated during stage one, on the innovation process, were explored in other research sites.

Stage one

A major part of the study focused on what our stage-one case studies considered to be their innovations and how they managed their innovations. In order to explore these issues the research adopted the comparative, longitudinal and processual case-study method from the organisational change literature (Pettigrew et al, 1988). This method was adopted and transposed into a study on innovation because it unlocked three key questions for innovation research:

- the 'what' of innovation or its content,
- the 'why' of innovation or its context, making a distinction between inner and outer context and noting the importance of engagement with the external environment to achieve innovation rather than change (Osborne, 1998), and,
- the 'how' of innovation, or an analysis of its processes.

This allowed the researchers to adopt a grounded approach to establish the nature and content of the case-study associations' innovations. This approach allowed the case-study associations to build pictures of their innovations. They were able to describe them, rather than impose preconceived answers and views of innovation in housing associations (Dean, 1987; Meyer and Goes, 1988; Wolfe, 1994), which the use of a questionnaire with many closed and restricted answers would have done. Categorisation of the innovations identified by the associations (presented in Chapter 4) followed over thirty semi-structured and group interviews with key, typically senior, members of each case-study organisation in the summer of 1997. These interviews explored: major organisational developments, typically over the five years prior to the study; the organisation; the background of the people being interviewed; and their understanding of the concept of innovation. The interviews also examined contextual information about the inner and outer environment to ascertain why the associations were developing their claimed innovations. These interviews focused upon senior organisational members, including board members and other key actors who were identified through a snowball sampling procedure in each association. A categorisation system was developed and the research team classified the innovations identified in each organisation independently and differences were discussed until a consensus was reached. They were also agreed with the collaborative case-study associations.

The analysis of the management of innovation or the 'how' question involved intensive fieldwork of about three months in each association, followed by monitoring. The researchers were in the field from the autumn of 1997 until the summer of 1998. A variety of data sources were used in these intensive case-studies. Inside the organisations semi-structured interviews were undertaken with staff from all levels of the hierarchy in order to gain different perspectives on the innovation process. In total some 130 interviews/group discussions were undertaken. These were made up of at least two board members from each association, all directors, nearly 50 middle managers and over 70 front-line staff. These interviews focused on actors reciting their 'innovation story' (whether current innovations or completed innovations) and the key phases in the 'innovation journey'. A range of documentary sources were also drawn upon, including minutes of board and working-group meetings, various internal reports, past and current plans, memoranda, and statistical data. This information was used to corroborate the dates of key events and gain insights into organisational life. In addition, observation, both informal in nature during the research visits, together with the formal attending of the board and other meetings supplemented these methods. Research interviews were conducted in a diversity of settings, giving a broader feel for the organisations being studied. Interviews were taped wherever possible. Key interviews were transcribed through the research period. Writing up the material and analysis has involved using keyword searches and detailed reading and matrix building of the evidence.

Because innovations do not always develop inside the organisation, research interviews were also undertaken with partner organisations. These included around thirty interviews with local authorities, voluntary groups and private sector suppliers for each case-study organisation. These interviews sought partners' perceptions of the organisation and their claimed innovations, and, where innovations were jointly developed, interviews were carried out as described above. In addition, national representative organisations were interviewed to establish a wider picture of innovation. Work with tenants focused on two group discussions in each organisation and the examination of documentation about the nature of communication. These discussion groups involved tenant representatives and tenants who were not formally involved in the consultation process.

The case-study housing associations

The three case-study associations were selected to represent the 'super-league' (Malpass, 1999) of around 200 associations owning more than 1,000 homes or 90% of the stock. The approach taken was to select associations that would allow for in-depth, intensive case-study work rather than to gain a representative sample of all associations and to employ extensive, questionnaire-based methods. Nevertheless, these associations were selected to capture some of the key aspects of all association activity. Consequently, the three associations differ in size, origin, location and provision. They were selected prior to the study commencing and the research brief being finalised. They played a role in the design of the research brief, identifying issues they wanted to see researched and played an ongoing role in the management and organisation of the research. They sat on the research advisory board that met throughout the project and played a role in understanding and interpreting the research findings. Findings were communicated back to them at relevant points during the research, which included an 'away day' to discuss results and seminars held in two of the associations to disseminate key aspects of the findings to a broader group of staff.

The first organisation, East Dorset Housing Association, owns around 3,000 homes near the south coast. It was one of the early Large Scale Voluntary Transfer (LSVT) associations transferring its stock in 1990. Some members of the council saw this as contributing towards the government's privatisation agenda whereas others saw it as an opportunity to reinvest in the stock and meet housing needs while escaping from a punitive financial regime. It remained spatially concentrated in its original authority boundaries until relatively recently. Its main provision is general needs and elderly accommodation. This type of association will come to dominate the sector during the next decade as stock transfers continue apace.

The second case, Riverside Housing Association, was established in the early part of the twentieth century and was a founder member of the forerunner of the National Housing Federation (the English umbrella organisation, representing the interests of housing associations) in the 1930s. It manages over 20,000 homes focusing upon general needs provision (one of the 15 largest associations). The majority of its stock is concentrated in the North West of England, though it increasingly owns and manages homes across the North and in the Midlands. Though founded earlier its major stock expansion dates from the late 1960s. It has a range of provision extending to special needs and ex-New Town stock. It developed a divisional structure during the 1990s and operates a network of devolved units akin to smaller associations.

Case three, Touchstone Housing Association, manages approximately 12,000 homes across a large geographical area, concentrated around the Midlands, with a number of regional offices. It was the product of a merger between Coventry Churches Housing Association and Nomid Housing Association in the early 1990s. Coventry Churches, the larger of the two previous organisations, was established under the auspices of the Coventry Council of Churches, in the late 1960s, in response to problems of urban deprivation. It has recently disposed of its residential care provision and focuses upon general needs stock. It also has a very large portfolio of low-cost homeownership provision, with a particular emphasis upon older people, which gives it a highly complex organisational structure.

Stage two

Stage one of the research provided information on the nature of housing association innovations, the reasons why they are developed and how the innovation process is managed. These findings were then exported into the wider housing association sector to examine the extent to which they held true in this wider setting. The classification systems developed in stage one were applied to the sector as a whole. Findings from this then were used to explore the innovation process in other settings and a wider range of housing associations. The new work sought to establish the determinants of organisational innovativeness. This involved developing explanations for statistical testing.

The project was intended to classify innovation in the sector through questionnaire surveys. However, this part of the work did not proceed because of problems of non-response across the sector: housing associations were being over-researched and were not responding to questionnaires, even when the industry regulator circulated or endorsed them! An alternative strategy was formulated based on bibliographic sources, an approach frequently adopted in the North American public services innovation literature (Borins, 2000; Golden, 1990). These bibliographic sources of reported innovations were used as the population for the remainder of the research. The value and applicability of this approach to researching public services innovation is demonstrated – we apply and develop the Literature-Based Innovation Output Indicator (LBIOI) from the private sector innovation literature (Coombs et al, 1996). This data set also serves as the basis for the research on organisational innovativeness and was used as the population to sample the additional cases where we explored the innovation process. The sample of associations selected for the innovation process research drew on different types of innovation and association. Further details of the methods adopted at the various stages of the project are described throughout the book.

Structure of the book

The findings from the authors' research are presented as a totality, and not in relation to each stage of the project. Where the findings are drawn from only one part of the project this is made clear. Before the empirical findings of the research and their implications for the management of innovation are drawn out, Chapter 2 explores the complex concept of innovation. Innovation is one of the most widely researched aspects of the social sciences. Rogers (1995) and Wolfe (1994) cite nearly 7,000 studies between them on innovation research. Consequently the review contained in Chapter 2 draws out issues of organisational and management innovation research relevant to this study. This includes the research themes of innovation diffusion, organisational innovativeness and process theory or the management of innovation. Chapter 3 introduces the case-study material for this report: housing associations. For those familiar with the housing association sector they may wish to skim the early parts of this section where we outline the nature, scale and scope of the sector and its diversification over recent years into what are referred to as 'non-core activities'. The chapter concludes by reviewing the relationship between innovation and regulation. Innovation and regulation are both about change, but very different types. Regulation is concerned with controlling organisations so that they change and behave in desired ways, one of which is to produce innovations. Innovation is concerned with discontinuous change. This tension is at the heart of the Labour government's reform programme for public services. For example, the local government BestValue regime is one that aims to achieve continuous improvement, or incremental innovation. It is also imposes a new regulatory regime on those parts of local government not previously exposed to inspection. Similarly associations have a new regulatory regime which exerts further control over them, raising questions about their innovative capacity.

In Chapter 4 the authors tackle the important question of innovation classification. Writers on innovation have repeatedly called for researchers to be clear about the nature and attributes of the innovations they study. This is important not only for innovation research, making it possible for findings to be generalised, but also for public policy and managers. Different types of innovation will require different managerial responses – if the nature of an innovation is not clearly spelt out innovation implementation may fail. In Chapter 4 a two-stage innovation classification system is devised, tested and applied to the case-study associations. The classification system is subsequently applied to the sector as a whole through the use of bibliographic techniques. The authors apply the Literature-Based Innovation Output Indicator (LBIOI) (Coombs et al, 1996) to illustrate the value of bibliographic techniques to the management of public services and public policy. Such techniques are highlighted as important in the age of 'evidence-based policy and practice', particularly because longitudinal databases can be used systematically to promote good practice.

Having established the housing association sector's innovative capacity and which housing associations are innovating, Chapter 5 goes on to discover if there are particular characteristics that define the 'innovative housing association'. Here we systematically research a range of factors such as management, size, functional differentiation, professionalism, geographical spread, specialisation and so on. The findings of this chapter indicate that there is an innovative housing association and that it has distinct characteristics. This has particular implications for the development of the sector given the current process of local authority transfers.

The way in which innovation is managed is discussed in Chapter 6. The research findings from this study support larger studies, typically undertaken in the USA and in the private sector, which indicate that the management of innovation is not a linear or straightforward process but rather an iterative journey of uncertainty. We draw upon the metaphor developed by Van de Ven et al (1999) of the 'innovation journey'. There are three key signposts through this journey: innovation initiation, innovation development and the implementation of innovations. A range of housing association practice in the management of innovation is presented in this chapter to illustrate the 'innovation journey' and lessons are extrapolated that highlight the importance of boundary scanning, teams, experiments, and so on, which form the basis of our recommendations. The book is drawn together in Chapter 7. The conclusions highlight innovation lessons and discuss the future nature of innovation in housing associations given the dawn of a new regulatory regime. The wider implications for other public services organisations are also drawn out.

Note

[1] The term housing association embraces a wide range of independent, private, not-for-profit organisations. More recently the sector has been designated the Registered Social Landlord (RSL) sector to capture this diversity and to account for the creation of Local Housing Companies and the diversification of the sector. These organisations provide rented and shared ownership accommodation to a variety of low-income households.

TWO

Public services innovation: perspectives on innovation in organisation and management

Innovation is a complex area of research and practice. It is about change, uncertainty, discontinuity and the implementation of new ways of working. Innovations can redefine the way we do business, for example moving away from face-to-face interactions to ones using information technology, or can lead to organisations working with new groups of users. Innovation can send organisations and sectors on new trajectories and open new routes on the innovation journey. It can also be about incremental change as organisations continuously improve their service quality over time. Innovation raises questions about the role of people and organisations, the ways in which some organisations adopt innovations while others do not, the nature of these innovative organisations and the ways in which organisations manage the innovation process from idea through to a new routine and way of working.

It is now imperative that public services organisations understand if they are either lead innovators or laggards. Consequently they need to be clear about the organisational characteristics which will increase the likelihood of them innovating and to understand how innovation is managed. There are a range of pressures requiring them to innovate: the modernisation agenda for public services, the changing environment, the changing expectations of users and so on. The issue of innovation is explored below – we define innovation and highlight some of the key areas of innovation knowledge that we have drawn upon. We present the management of innovation as a journey of discovery and uncertainty (Van de Ven et al, 1989, 1999). Having done this we move on to the important question of innovation classification and measurement and present a two-stage classification system. Clear classification of innovation is necessary for managers to understand the organisational needs and requirements that different innovations may pose. Initially we turn to the definition of innovation.

Defining innovation

The introduction to this book noted the increased use of the term 'innovation' in public management, social policy and the housing association sector in particular. This section briefly reviews the extensive organisational studies literature on innovation. Innovation is one of the most widely researched phenomena in the social sciences and now has a vast literature. For example, Everett Rogers' (1995) work on the diffusion of innovations cites over 5,000 studies on this topic alone, while Richard Wolfe's (1994) computerised citation index search revealed nearly 2,000 articles containing the words organisational or organisation and innovation in the five-year period ending in 1994. A reading of this diverse literature on innovation indicates that it is a highly complex concept. It is not therefore possible to offer a discrete definition. Rather a range of dimensions characterised by innovation can be drawn out. It:

- is a process, through which new ideas, objects and practices are created, developed or reinvented (Rogers, 1995; Kimberly, 1981);
- relates to the introduction and application of ideas within a role, group or organisation (King, 1992);
- is most commonly associated with processes, products or procedures, or outcomes (Abernathy et al, 1983);
- is something new and novel to the relevant unit of adoption, rather than newness per se (Aitken and Hage, 1971; Hage and Dewar, 1973; Rogers, 1995);
- is designed with the intent to benefit the individual, the group, organisation or wider society (Hosking and Morley, 1991; Anderson and King, 1991; Hosking and Anderson, 1992) though an innovation may have a negative and unanticipated impact (Osborne, 1998);
- finally, and importantly, it is associated with discontinuous change, framebreaking rather than framebending (Tushman and Anderson, 1986; Tushman and Nadler, 1996; Osborne, 1998) and a process of creative destruction.

The breadth of the concept is captured within the diversity of innovation research. Slappendel's (1996) chronological analysis traces innovation organisational research through key social science traditions. She highlights how early research saw innovation as the result of individual action. It sought to characterise the traits of innovative people and put forward ideas about the innovation champion, the leader and the entrepreneur. This period of research is associated with the early work of Everett Rogers (1962) and has been based on cross-sectional surveys. As social sciences developed through the 1960s and 1970s and came to focus on the environment, so the structuralist perspectives associated with Marxism and the sociology of the functionalists came to dominate innovation research. This work served to stress the importance of the wider organisational environment in the innovation process and highlighted factors such as organisational size, complexity, differentiation, formalisation, centralisation and strategic type. It again relied upon cross-sectional surveys and one of its key proponents will be discussed again below in relation to the work in this report on innovation process theory, Zaltman et al (1973). As social science research has more widely sought to reconcile these two aspects – agency or people and structure or the environment – so innovation research has developed its own 'interactive process' perspective. This relatively recent development sees innovation produced by the interaction of structural influences and the actions of individuals. It does not view innovation as static and an objectively defined object or practice (as the two previous perspectives do) but rather something perceived by the unit of adoption, be that a person, team or organisation. It also draws attention to the way in which innovations are reinvented through their adoption and implementation. It adopts the intensive methods of case-studies and case histories, as opposed to the extensive survey methods mentioned above. In a similar vein Wolfe's (1994) overview of organisational innovation research notes three research themes: diffusion, organisational innovativeness, and process theory. These are of particular interest to public services organisations and each area will be reviewed.

Innovation diffusion

Innovation diffusion is concerned with the diffusion of innovations through a population of potential adopter organisations over time and/ or space. The cumulative adoption of innovation over time is depicted as a horizontal S-shaped curve when an innovation's saturation point is reached. Early adopters are represented as innovators and later adopters as laggards. Key questions are concerned with explaining the rate of adoption over time and/or space. A range of factors have been found to influence innovation diffusion, the majority of which is derived from North American studies with few examples within Britain. Where there is British literature it is often normative, promoting models as innovation diffusion change agents (for example Stewart, 1996), applies concepts to secondary data in a general manner (for example Harrow and Willcocks, 1992), or considers diffusion as part of a wider study (Osborne, 1998). Consequently, there is little known about the diffusion of innovation and factors influencing adoption from a British perspective. The North American literature on both public policy innovation and management innovation, on the other hand, does identify a number of significant factors that affect adoption rates. However, much of this literature only concerns itself with the adoption of technical innovations in, for example, hospitals (Kimberly and Evanisko, 1981).

The most comprehensively developed model of innovation diffusion is that of Everett Rogers (1995) who has documented more than 3,000 studies from the public and private sectors, from individuals, organisations and communities. Rogers develops an innovation adoption model with five variables that determine the rate of adoption – the relative speed with which members of a social system adopt an innovation.

First, the characteristics of innovations have been shown to be important in many studies and to influence the adoption and nature of an innovation because not all innovations are equivalent units of analysis, or equivalent 'products' for adopting organisations (for example see Damanpour, 1991; Osborne, 1998; Walker and Jeanes, 2001; Wolfe, 1994). Rogers (1995, pp 15-16) argues that the characteristics of innovations, as perceived by the adopter, help to explain their differential rate of adoption. He identifies the most influential innovation characteristics as the innovation's relative advantage, compatibility, complexity, trialability and observability.

The second explanatory variable is the type of innovation decision. The social system within which the innovation is to be adopted can influence the likelihood of adoption through the types of decision that can be taken. Optional innovation decisions are choices to adopt or reject an innovation. These decisions are made by individual actors within the social system and are independent of other members of the system. Collective innovation decisions are where the members of a social system adopt or reject an innovation by consensus. Authority innovation decisions "are choices to adopt or reject an innovation that are made by a relatively few individuals in a system who possess power, status or technical expertise" (Rogers, 1995, p 29). Authority innovation decisions are frequently encountered by public services organisations.

Third, communication channels refer to the methods by which innovations are made known to potential adopters and the information-exchange relationships between different actors.

Fourth, Rogers (1995, p 23) defines a social system as 'a set of interrelated units that are engaged in joint problem-solving to accomplish common goals'. It is argued that the nature of the social system will again influence the rate of adoption. Factors influencing this include: the social structure, the patterned social relationship of members of the unit of analysis; system effects where the influences of the structure and/or composition of a system affect the behaviour of the members of the system; and norms and values, the established behaviour patterns of members of the social system.

Fifth, change agents' promotional efforts are seen as critical in influencing innovation decisions towards the innovation and influencing 'opinion leaders'.

There are a number of weaknesses in Rogers' work, and diffusion research more broadly, that need to be noted. First, Rogers' emphasis is upon individuals rather than organisations and findings from research into individual people are read across into organisations in his model. Thus in the above model change agents are accorded a major role and are often described as 'people persuading other people'. Second, the adoption model is presented as a linear innovation–decision process with the following stages: (1) knowledge; (2) persuasion; (3) decision; (4) implementation; and (5) confirmation. However, as noted above, innovation is an iterative process, thus it has been argued that we need to pay more attention to the evaluation stage of innovation adoption (Mohr, 1987) and understand that though innovation may have identifiable steps they are not necessarily sequential (Van de Ven et al, 1989).

Rogers nonetheless does offer us some important lessons for the management of innovation:

- different types of innovation, as described by their characteristics, require different management skills and techniques, which will vary within and between organisations;
- the adoption of innovation frequently involves reinvention during the implementation of innovation. Indeed Rogers goes as far as to argue that reinvention is necessary to ensure that an innovation is matched to its local setting and ownership is taken of the innovation by its implementers, irrespective of whether the innovation is adopted or tailor-made.

Organisational innovativeness

The second theme is organisational innovativeness research. This seeks to discover the determinants of an organisation's propensity to innovate. This work has focused on organisations rather than individuals. The approach typically involves innovations being externally defined (Kimberly and Evanisko, 1981) and organisations being given scores of the number of innovations that they have adopted. The research techniques are then quantitative as researchers seek to explain the different number of innovations adopted. There are examples of these themes being applied to public services organisations, for example, Rogers and Kim (1985) on the diffusion of innovations, Osborne's (1998) exploration of diffusion and organisational innovativeness and Damanpour's (1991) study of the adoption of technological innovations.

The lessons to emerge from these studies is that characteristics such as the role of specialist staff, professional staff and large organisations are significant in describing the innovative organisation.

The management of innovation theory

The third stream is concerned with the management of innovation and is referred to as innovation process theory. This seeks to understand how and why innovations emerge, develop, grow to become 'routine', or terminate. Two schools have been distinguished: rational or staged (for example Zaltman et al, 1973) and process models (for example Schroeder et al, 1989). Rational models are "composed of a set of stages or phases ordered along the temporal dimensions of their anticipated sequence" (Zaltman et al, 1973, p 52). Authors typically identify two main stages: initiation and implementation. This staged model portrays innovations sequentially unfolding over time with a general pattern of innovation. Following the development of an innovation idea the process runs sequentially through nine stages:

1) the decision-making unit becomes *aware* of innovation existence;
2) the problem or opportunity is *matched* to the innovation;
3) innovation costs and benefits are *appraised*;
4) sources of support and/or opposition attempt to *influence* the innovation;
5) a decision is made to *adopt or reject* the innovation;

6) the innovation is *implemented*;
7) the innovation decision is reviewed and *confirmed or reversed*;
8) the innovation becomes adopted as *routine*; and,
9) the innovation becomes *infused* or fully applied.

This research has highlighted the fact that innovations do have key stages. However, though limited in number, studies either do not fully support these ideas or support them only in relation to the least radical, small-scale innovations (King, 1992; Pelz, 1983). This has resulted in the innovation process being cast as iterative, complex and multidirectional:

> ... from among the innovations that were charted ... we can say that the innovation journey can be accomplished in a number of different ways and can unfold along many different routes. Whatever route is taken, the innovation journey crosses a rugged landscape that is highly ambiguous, if often uncontrollable, and involves a good deal of luck. (Van de Ven et al, 1999, p 65)

This view of innovation management has been developed over the last twenty years in a series of longitudinal research studies led by Andrew Van de Ven. In a number of papers Van de Ven and others (Schroeder et al, 1989; Angle and Van de Ven, 1989; Van de Van et al, 1999), argue that there are not stages but key observations that can be made about three temporal periods in the innovation journey:

- initiation,
- development, and
- implementation or termination.

These common elements were derived from empirical observations in the Minnesota Innovation Research Program. The dozen common patterns of the innovation journey are summarised below and are "expected to be more pronounced for innovations of greater novelty, size, and temporal duration" (Van de Ven et al, 1999, p 25).

First, the initiation of innovations involves three stages: gestation, 'shocks', and resource plans. Innovations are the product of periods of 'gestation' which are often the result of coincidences rather than opportunistic responses by single entrepreneurs to dramatic incidents. Second, innovation is stimulated by 'shocks' or 'triggers', often following a period of gestation. Consequently the initiation of an innovation can be internal or external in origin, for example new leadership, loss of market share or performance gaps. Third, initiation comes to an end once plans are submitted to resource controllers to launch the innovation into its developmental stage.

The developmental period involves a large number of processes. Fourth, innovation proliferates into several ideas and activities. Proliferation occurs because:

- Innovation is an ambiguous and uncertain process; specific outcomes are not known until all avenues have been explored.
- Families of products or procedures may be simultaneously developed to ensure viability or to reduce risk.
- Different mechanisms govern proliferation; activities governed by institutional rules tend to follow a unitary sequence of stages; activities governed by goals and plans tend initially to diverge then subsequently converge.

Fifth, setbacks occur because plans do not develop as anticipated or environmental change alters the context for the innovation; however, they can be the basis for learning as resources and schedules are re-collaborated. Sixth, success criteria for innovations alter over time as the various stakeholders' perception of success criteria change. In particular, differences occur between resource controllers and innovation managers, which diverge over time and can result in power struggles. Seventh, the innovation team, typically comprised of people involved on a part-time basis, experiences turnover and differing levels of commitment and excitement about the innovation. Eighth, top managers play crucial, if changing, roles throughout the innovation process. They both solve problems and ensure that innovation remains on track. Ninth and tenth, the development of innovation involves developing relationships with other organisations that can change the nature of the innovation as partnerships involve processes of renegotiation, resulting in unanticipated outcomes. They also involve working with a range of organisations, for example government, regulators, trade associations, to create the infrastructure for supporting innovation development and implementation.

Innovations reach the end of the journey when they are implemented or terminated. Eleventh, adoption and implementation is an ongoing process as new ideas coexist with old practices that over time become integrated or the innovation is reinvented to suit the local situation. Finally, innovation stops when it is either fully implemented or when resources run out. Innovation literature often focuses upon the innovation initiation and development stage and does not fully consider implementation or the 'sustaining of innovation'. The implementation and sustaining of innovation is taken to mean that targeted employees become committed to an innovation and use it appropriately (Klein and Sorra, 1996).

The model, depicted in Figure 1, assumes an organisation is proceeding in the direction of *A* (a time continuum). At time zero a shock occurs, following a period of gestation, that propels the innovation in the direction of point *B*. The innovation then is moving in the direction of *B*, while the organisation is moving in the direction of *A*. The process of innovation development, when real efforts are taken to transform the idea into something concrete, will result in proliferation and, as long as the new ideas are loosely related, will continue moving in the direction of *B*. 'Setbacks or surprises' can lead to temporary setbacks, with ideas 'put on the shelf' or projects aborted. As the innovation develops it starts to be implemented, integrating with other innovations and/or old processes, as illustrated by the linkages between the innovation and the *A*-time continuum. These tend to take three forms: (1) the old organisation can be moved towards point *B*, while the entire organisation fundamentally changes direction as a result of the innovation; or (2) the innovation can be moved towards point *A* and blended into the old organisation; or (3) the old and new can coexist in parallel progression with linkages between the old and the new. In addition to the restructuring of the organisation to meet the needs of the innovation and new working practices, hands-on top management will generally take place throughout the organisation's route to point *B* if innovation implementation is to be successfully achieved or an innovation is terminated or abandoned. This process-based approach to innovation offers major advantages by highlighting the non-rational nature of decision making, the political context within which innovations are introduced and the iterative, dynamic and changing nature of innovation.

When undertaking research on innovation, or seeking to answer management questions within an organisation, it is important to be clear what type of question is being asked. For example, an organisation could be concerned about its relatively late adoption of innovation compared to its competitors. The writings on innovation diffusion would offer clues to this question. Alternatively a chief executive may

Figure I: The innovation process model

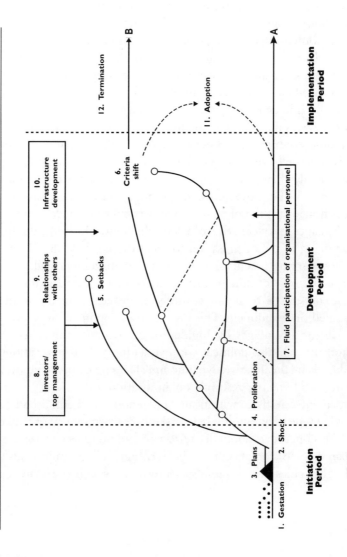

Source: Adapted from Van de Ven et al (1999)

want to ensure that he or she is creating an organisation with innovative capacity and would look to the lessons from the organisational innovativeness literature. Finally, an organisation may wish to improve its management of innovation and look to the innovation process theory literature. This book takes two sets of this theory: that on organisational innovativeness and the management of innovation, and that on process theory. Though they have very different origins and seek to answer very different questions they are both important areas in which to build up our knowledge of public services innovation. Our process research is concerned with the whole process from initiation to implementation and how it was managed. Work on organisational innovativeness is concerned not with the adoption of an innovation, as this may merely mean that an organisation is committed to using an innovation, but to its actual use within an organisation. This may preclude full implementation, as an organisation may still be developing and exploring the use of an innovation but has dedicated resources to this, such that an active decision has been taken. Given the complexity of innovation, clear innovation classification needs to be developed for innovation knowledge (both practical and academic) to be utilised. We now explore the innovation characteristics in this study and specify them.

Classifying innovation

Given the complexity of innovation, calls have been made for clear innovation classification to develop innovation research knowledge and enhance the practice of managing innovation (for example King and Anderson, 1995; Rogers, 1995; Wolfe, 1994). The variety of approaches to innovation research outlined above suggests that innovations and innovators will have many different attributes and characteristics and that these need to be made explicit if we are to understand the potential varying trajectories that different innovations will offer in different organisational contexts. However, many attempts to classify innovations have typically relied upon two-dimensional categories or dichotomies, for example, Damanpour and Evan's (1984) technical-administrative classification. Wolfe (1994) argues that it is important for researchers to specify the attributes of innovation as a starting point for understanding innovation and generalising research results. His review of innovation research identifies 17 innovation attributes that can be used in the process of classifying and understanding innovations that have been influential in other innovation research. By contrast Rogers (1995) offers the five characteristics outlined above. Though providing a range of dimensions to innovation, the potential list of attributes could allow for an eclectic, unspecified and subjective classification of innovation. For example, King and Anderson (1995) highlight socio-technical innovation characteristics, innovation characteristics and innovation source as key classification criteria but offer no guidance as to how such frameworks should be used. Whipp and Clark (1986) provide a more useful categorisation that moves from strategic innovations through to cosmetic change. Similarly Rogers (1995) does not offer a critical review of the innovation literature in arriving at his five characteristics, for example there is no methodological review of the papers cited in his text. This work nonetheless indicates the varying significance an innovation can have on an organisation, differences between innovations and between innovation and change. Moreover, it serves to indicate the lack of accepted typologies of innovation and their attributes.

Recent work by Stephen Osborne (1998) has helped to bring clarity to this debate. Osborne has developed a two-dimensional typology of innovation building upon the traditional separation of innovations as product or process. Following Normann (1991) he contends that social policy organisations develop innovations that are simultaneously product and process because services are typically consumed at the point of production. The separation of product and process in the innovation literature developed from literature on organisational life cycles. This argues that new organisations are seen to produce product innovation while older, mature organisations produce process innovations to enhance the technical efficiency of previous product innovations. However, such a perspective denies the possibility of 'reinvention' and the impact of discontinuities in organisations or across sectors (Tushman and Anderson, 1986). In response to concerns about over-simplistic life cycle

Figure 2: A typology of public services innovation

		USERS	
		New	**Existing**
	New	Total innovation	Evolutionary
SERVICES			
	Existing	Expansionary	Developmental

Source: Adapted from Osborne (1998)

perspectives Osborne (1998) draws on the work of Abernathy et al (1983) to develop an innovation typology. He argues that organisations can 'de-mature' and move away from the 'mature' productivity/efficiency focus, which often relates to standardisation, to focus upon product development and diversity, which is seen to be typical of organisations earlier in the life cycle. Osborne's typology explicitly explores the interrelationship between product and process, allows for product or process innovations to occur at any stage of the life cycle and highlights discontinuity (innovation) and continuity (organisational development). Figure 2 presents this typology as a two-by-two matrix. The left-hand side of the matrix is concerned with the impact of organisational change upon the services that an agency produces, categorising them as existing or new ones that involve 'service discontinuity'. The top of the matrix is concerned with the relationship of an organisational change to the organisation's users. Again it seeks to categorise the relationship to clients as meeting the needs of existing end-user groups, or new ones, which involves 'end-user discontinuity'. Central in this typology and definition of innovation is that innovation is concerned with discontinuity in services, either to end users or both.

This two-dimensional typology leads to four types of organisational change:

(1) total innovation, involving discontinuous change which is both new to the organisation, or may even be the creation of a new organisation itself, and serves a new user group;
(2) expansionary innovation, where the change involves offering an existing service of the organisation to a new user group;
(3) evolutionary innovation, where the change involves providing a new service to the existing user group of an organisation;
(4) developmental or incremental innovation, where the services of an organisation to its existing user group are modified or improved.

Osborne (1998) presents data to describe innovative activity and estimate its extent among the voluntary and non-profit, personal, social services organisations. His findings indicate that about half his sample did not undertake any innovative activity though claiming to do so, while just over a third developed service innovations with the remainder developing existing services under the banner of innovation.

This typology of innovation is a useful classification mechanism that allows innovations to be identified as development or a continuation of existing activities – framebending – or expanding existing services into new markets or to new user groups or both – framebreaking. This is important for understanding the needs in the organisation. Total innovations will require new skills and a different approach to management. Other public services institutions, such as regulators, would be unlikely to be concerned with developmental activities because they are minor modifications or improvements and represent continuity. Conversely, a total innovation may challenge the very basis of a regulatory framework leading to the need for adjustment.

Osborne's typology identifies the key attributes of innovations for social policy organisations. By focusing upon the two dimensions of users and services the typology excludes other innovation attributes that may be significant. For example, an expansionary or evolutionary innovation may be radical or affect the entire organisation and require the acquisition of the new skills Osborne suggests are needed for total innovations. Conversely it is possible for a total innovation not to be radical or only affect part of the organisation. This suggests that additional specification of the attributes of innovations is needed. Downs and Mohr (1976) suggest that primary and secondary innovation characteristics need to be identified. Osborne's typology indicates the primary innovative characteristics for organisations meeting social policy objectives. Secondary attributes are dependent upon the perception of organisational members and may vary from organisation to organisation. Given the lack of agreed innovation characteristics, the six attributes that Wolfe (1994) found to influence innovation in previous research are adopted and their validity explored in this study. Table 1 describes these attributes and the dimensions on which they are measured.

Conclusions

Given the complexity of innovation and the continually escalating requirement for innovation in public services it is important that members of public services organisations are clear about their organisational and management innovation needs. These fall around the themes of diffusion and may lead to questions such as: why are we not leading an innovative organisation? They may wish to know what the characteristics of innovative organisations are in their sector. They may also wish to develop knowledge about the management of innovation. Our work now goes on to explore these latter two questions in the housing association sector. Prior to this we introduce readers to the sector and the past and future factors which are driving innovation.

Table 1: Secondary innovation attribute definitions

Attribute	Measurement scale	Definition
Adaptability	Flexible versus inflexible	The ability to refine, elaborate and modify an innovation according to the needs and objectives of the implementer
Centrality	Central versus peripheral	The degree to which an innovation concerns the major day-to-day work of the organisation and involves activities critical to organisational performance
Organisational focus	Technical versus administrative	The aspect of the organisation to which the innovation is most relevant
Pervasiveness	Low to high	The proportion of total behaviours occurring within an organisation that are expected to be affected by the innovation; pervasiveness is a function of how many organisational members are expected to change their behaviours due to the innovation and how much time these people will spend behaving in new ways
Radicalness	Low to high	The extent to which an innovation represents technological changes and thus implies new behaviours for organisational subsystems and/or members
Uncertainty	Low to high	Knowledge concerning the link between the innovation's inputs, processes, and outcomes

Source: Adapted from Wolfe (1994, p 419)

THREE

The housing association policy environment, regulation and innovation

This chapter introduces our case-study public services sector: housing associations. Here we discuss the changing nature, scale and scope of the housing association sector and focus on diversification and the medium-term environment. This policy analysis will be used as a backdrop to give context to the debate about the innovative capacity of housing associations and to explore the pressures and external forces that may be driving innovation. The chapter closes with a discussion of the relationship between innovation and regulation. This is a particularly pertinent area of public services policy given the exhortation by governments to innovate within a field where there has been a concomitant increase in the regulation of public services. This has increased, not abated, under the Labour administration. The Best Value programme illustrates this tension with its requirements for innovation or continuous improvement within a highly regulated framework that adopts the regulatory tool of inspection together with sanctions and intervention. The housing association regulatory regime is currently being expanded to adopt aspects of the Best Value approach to local government management.

The nature, scale and scope of English housing associations

Nature

The promotion of housing associations as the providers of new social housing has altered their nature, as often specialist but complementary providers to local authorities, to give them a specific general needs remit. These changes were part of a wider social policy process which led to the introduction of market mechanisms (Le Grand and Bartlett, 1993), organisational decentralisation (Pollitt et al, 1998) and increased regulation (Hood et al, 1999) in education, health, community care and housing. The social housing 'quasi-market' was initially production-focused: introducing greater competition between associations for fixed government subsidy together with private finance in the development process, thereby transferring risk from government to associations (see Cope, 1998, for a more detailed discussion of the pre- and post-1988 Housing Act financial regime). Though not representing the full extent of a free market, the social housing quasi-market was seen to develop rapidly during the 1990s (Bramley, 1993) and more comprehensively than other sectors (Le Grand and Bartlett, 1993). Its development has continued apace as council housing is transferred into the association sector (Walker, 2000), and as more associations compete for scarce resources. This process is set to continue. The Labour government promises to increase transfer rates to 200,000 units a year (DETR, 2000), which is leading to predictions that council housing will have all but disappeared by 2010 (Bright, 2000).

Risk was also passed to associations in the ongoing management and maintenance of their homes (for a more detailed discussion see Walker and Smith, 1999). Associations now have to plan their future maintenance responsibilities based upon the sinking funds they establish and the likely prospects of remortgaging the homes in their stock. Management and maintenance allowances are a thing of the past because what matters is the ability to let a home in a decent state of repair as quickly as possible to ensure that loans can be repaid to the financial institutions. Associations now use tools such as option appraisal to establish the relative value of improvement compared with the disposal of an asset. Treasury management, ensuring the availability of funds both for development and future maintenance, is now of vital importance to all but the smallest association. These factors have enhanced the significance of the finance department. In particular, attention to cash flow has become a predominant feature for finance departments. If cash flow illustrates the short-term risk associations now face, there are also long-term ones. For example, transfer associations (Large Scale Voluntary Transfers or Local Housing Companies) may have taken out long-term finance at a time of high interest rates. They may be long-term disadvantaged compared to other associations. Transfer associations may be locked into higher cost financial systems and be subject to penalities to be released from them in contrast to others who have floating rate finance and are not as highly indebted. Again treasury management is a major feature of housing association activity, with complex financial instruments being used to hedge against interest rate movements. The introduction of private finance brought associations into contact with a range of lenders whose influence over associations is now significant.

The production role was firmly embedded in the housing association sector through the curtailment of local authorities' role as providers of new social housing through the 1989 Local Government and Housing Act, which identified their new role as 'enabling authorities' (Goodlad, 1993). Housing associations are clearly one of the partners local authorities work with. Associations have moved from an agnostic relationship with local authorities in the early 1990s to building a range of partnerships, both formal and informal (Reid, 1995, 1999). This is partly a product of the changing environment, notably the gradual shift towards regeneration under the Conservative administration and the clear embracing of this under Labour, with the emphasis upon social exclusion, and the current vogue for partnership working.

Customers were notionally given a role in the new market. Government has encouraged associations to develop more responsive and customer-focused services (Housing Corporation, 1998a). Welfare-dependent customers could shop between providers to ensure value for money by using Housing Benefit as a 'voucher' and could negotiate rent levels, as the landlord and tenant agreed the newly introduced assured rents. Because demand exceeded supply in the early 1990s, tenants took what they were offered by a housing association landlord at the price suggested. More recently, and for a range of complex reasons, the associations' supply of customers has dwindled. Market pressures have been seen from other directions beyond those of production with associations now competing for tenants as low demand becomes a problem for many regions outside the South East of England (Cole et al, 1999).

This policy reform, into a new competitive environment, has fundamentally altered the behaviour of associations (Mullins et al, 2001). Notable here has been the emphasis placed on core business property management processes (rent collection, allocations and repairs) and the tensions between this form of behaviour and the welfare people-oriented processes which are once again identified as important (Walker, 2000). The impact of these policy changes, their interpretation in organisations and the ways in which they are changing organisational behaviour, has only started to be explored relatively recently (Walker and Smith, 1999; Mullins and Riseborough, 2000; Mullins et al, 2001) but not in relation to innovation. Though their behaviour may have changed, debate continues over their status as public, private and independent or voluntary organisations.

In order that housing associations could borrow on the private markets the Treasury defined them as private bodies – in this way their private finance expenditure does not count against government debt. Housing associations are independent organisations; they can go bankrupt and out of business. The notion of independence was strongly upheld at the time of the quasi-market reforms (Langstaff, 1992) and subsequently as they have diversified their activities (Mullins, 1997a). While they are private, independent organisations they are also voluntary and public. Their voluntary status is reflected in their various constitutional forms, which limit the ability to return profits to shareholders, and in board members serving in an unpaid capacity. As independent organisations delivering public services their governance arrangements have been investigated in some depth (Ashby, 1997). Their publicness comes from their funding arrangements. Though public production subsidies fell during the late 1990s, they have been rising recently. Many of the non-stock transfer associations have been largely funded by the public purse (see Ashworth et al, 2001, for an example in the Welsh context). Given the low incomes of many housing association tenants in any type of association (transfer or 'traditional'), Housing Benefit pays a large proportion of their day-to-day running costs – indirectly increasing their reliance on government subsidies. Indeed a number of studies have highlighted the importance of Housing Benefit to association survival. The various definitions which can be accorded to associations are used to their own ends. For example, during the debate on the 1995 White Paper, associations were able to work collectively as public and voluntary organisations with their funding body to rebuff government attempts to bring private sector developers into the 'public production subsidy regime' (Mullins, 1997b). Housing associations are clearly public services organisations. Though they are constitutionally and legally independent, they have high levels of public subsidy historically and currently invested in them and fulfil public policy goals.

The eclectic use of their public, private and voluntary forms by housing associations reflects wider debates about the ownership of organisations. Bozeman (1987) argues that all organisations are public, with variations along the three dimensions of ownership, funding and control. The ownership of a housing association is clearly private; however, as noted above, much of their funding is public. Though they are privately controlled by an independent board, the nature and extent of regulation, or external control, is sufficiently high to put them at the public end of the continuum. However, though the extent of publicness may vary, commentators increasingly find similarities between public, private and not-for-profit sectors. Boyne (2001: forthcoming) does not find any clear evidence of the distinctiveness of the management of public organisations, supporting earlier findings on the NHS (Pettigrew et al, 1992), while Mullins notes in a review of housing association merger activity that "it is difficult to deflect significant differences in the behaviour of non-profit and profit distributing business" (Mullins, 1999, p 352). Our argument is that housing associations can be referred to as public organisations, but they are able to occupy different ground on the dimensions of public, private and voluntary.

Scale

The scale of the sector has increased as it has taken on its new responsibilities. There are now over 1.3 million housing association homes in England, an increase of nearly 500,000 during the 1990s. Housing associations now represent 20% of all social housing in England and 5% of the total stock. Though the provision of new social housing has been important in this, much of the growth has come through the acquisition of local authority housing stock. Local authorities have been busy transferring their stock into the housing association sector to access resources that are denied to them as public sector bodies (Mullins et al, 1993). These processes of expansion and transfer are bringing further changes to the nature and scope of the sector. If all local authority stock is transferred by 2010, as some commentators have predicted, it will have increased the sector from 500,000 homes to nearly 5 million in less than two decades.

Scope

The scope of associations' work has always been broad and it is characterised by diversity of providers and provision (Cope, 1998). This diversity can be illustrated by research that sought to identify peer groups of associations in the early 1990s for the purposes of measuring comparative performance (Walker, 1994). Of the 2,200 registered associations, 370 owned nearly 95% of all homes, leaving 1,800 associations owning 70,000 homes – an average of nearly 39 homes per association. Many of these smaller associations have no paid staff and may use larger associations to manage their property, while others may be fully mutual cooperatives, almshouses or specialist small-scale providers of homes for older people, such as Abbeyfields. Consequently the scope of housing associations is difficult to capture below the larger ones.

In relation to their provision some associations specialise in their user group, for example serving only older people or young people or people with 'special needs' or households disadvantaged in the housing market, while others will provide homes for 'general needs families' yet combine this with other forms of more specialist provision. In addition to this some associations may be involved in the provision of various forms of low-cost home ownership. This complexity of providers and provision, together with the data available, meant that it was not possible to capture the variety of the sector clearly (Walker, 1994).

More recently, work by Malpass (1997) has attempted to capture the range of association activity by identifying four 'waves of formation' of associations. This serves to indicate that there is a diversity of origin of associations and illustrates the importance of social, economic and political factors in the public policy arena. The 'waves' also serve to indicate ways in which the sector and organisations have been reinvented through its ongoing life cycle. Malpass (1997) identifies the final wave of associations as the local authority stock transfer associations, who have transferred their whole housing stock or elements of it. These associations are very different from the more traditional associations in that they own large estates, which are concentrated in particular localities, and are typically family housing. Approximately 110 local authorities have transferred their entire stock and there is an ongoing programme of estate transfers. Consequently, of the 470 larger associations 110, or over 20% of all associations, have entered the sector in the last decade and represent a major reinvention in the sector, exemplifying discontinuity and establishing new trajectories.

If the range of constitutional forms and governance arrangements were already multifaceted, recent changes have increased their complexity. The 1996 Housing Act, which introduced the term Registered Social Landlords (RSLs) to capture its increased complexity, legislated for a new type of organisation, the Local Housing Company. These organisations differ from other housing associations in their constitution, relationships with other bodies, notable local authorities and their board membership, which can be up to one third local authority members and is usually one third tenants, with the remainder community representatives. Many older associations have been bringing tenants on to their boards for some time.

The 1988 Housing Act projected associations into the limelight of social policy as independent organisations which would solve a range of housing and public policy problems. However, this quickly led to a torrid time for them; expansion has come at a price. After being seen as the saviour of large and bureaucratic local authority landlords who were increasingly housing 'problem' households, associations came to be cast in a similar vein. They were seen to gather poor households in particular localities, and were condemned by John Redwood, the Welsh Secretary of State, for housing concentrations of lone parents. The government-backed venture into the owner-occupied sector, to help kick-start a depressed housing market in the early 1990s, also backfired as associations were perceived to be housing antisocial neighbours in owner-occupied communities and damaging house prices. If their image was changing from saviour to villain it was to deteriorate as government funding reduced from the mid-1990s and the wider environment in which they operated changed (for example Ford and Wilcox, 1994; Wagstaff, 1997). The outcome of these few illustrative pressures has been that associations have had to become highly responsive to the immediate and the national environment.

Diversification

From 1993 onwards, as government finance reduced, associations slowly became less dependent upon central government subsidy and more dependent upon private finance, and have now diversified their activities (Mullins and Riseborough, 2000). This exposed them to new users, services and markets. However, these pressures have not just been financial. The Page (1993) report highlighted the fact that the new financial regime for housing associations was producing pockets of severe deprivation and excessive concentrations of both particular household types and unemployed households. These deprived households were also more likely to be disconnected from the wider community and the services that they needed because they were housed on greenfield sites on the periphery of towns and cities. Thus there has been real pressure for change among housing associations as they come to grips with their new mainstream role. One facet of this search for new forms of activity is related to the attitudes within the sector towards organisational growth. It was assumed that associations would carry on growing and needed to, it was their *raison d'étre* – indeed that the attitude of many managers was 'develop or die'. Thus, as development resources dried up, new alternative furrows had to be ploughed.

The new furrow has been labelled diversification and it has taken two main paths. The first has been concerned with the development of welfare services and the second with profit-making ventures that seek to underwrite the cost of the social activity. Welfare services have been labelled 'housing plus', that is core property management services plus other activities. Though this is an ill-defined concept it is seen to have three strands (Housing Corporation, 1997). First, the creation and maintenance of sustainable communities is emphasised to overcome the difficulties alluded to above. Second, the investment made in social housing, through both investment in new building and the ongoing maintenance and management of the stock, is seen as a resource that can be made available to the local community. This may be either through 'local labour schemes', where local residents are employed by building contractors on trainee or permanent posts, or through the establishment of local firms to undertake maintenance. The final aspect is seen to be about partnerships with local stakeholders in communities. A range of initiatives has been identified in other research (Clapham and Evans, 1998) including: employment and training; care and support; youth schemes; participation; and specific projects such as furniture, health and transport services. These individual projects have been adopted by some associations as the basis of their new identity. For example, the arrival of regeneration as the centrepiece of housing policy over the past five years has led to many associations re-branding themselves as 'regeneration agencies' and the 'ideal partner for renewal projects'. Others have emphasised their care and support aspects. Mullins (1997a; Mullins and Riseborough, 2000) argues that these changes in identity are taking place as associations are jockeying for position in the new competitive (Reid, 1999) and uncertain housing association sector. One facet of this changing housing association scene is the advent of mergers and group structures as associations seek to expand without developing new homes and transfer organisations search for financially secure futures (Mullins, 1999).

This latter point is linked to the second characteristic of diversification. Housing associations have faced difficulties in financing 'housing plus' activities. They are not core business activities, and are risky and expensive while no government programme funds them. Therefore it is difficult to fund them from rental income, which is earmarked and under constant downward pressure to ensure that housing association homes remain affordable. The alternative is through reserves, but these are typically allocated for specific future expenditure, such as maintenance, and are not evenly held across the sector. Associations have therefore sought to develop profit-making activities. This has included developing student accommodation with universities, and more recently they have been involved in Private Finance Initiatives, for the NHS for example, and have been providing and/or developing market rented housing. These activities are also seen to help with the image of associations, indicating that they have a range of products and do not house solely those in greatest need. The profits from these activities are covenanted back to underwrite the costs of social activities. Many of those activities are undertaken in ways outside the core housing associations – this protects them against risk and allows a range of potentially diminimus activities to be undertaken. Group structures have been developed to manage this process.

This brief summary illustrates a sector in transformation. This transformation is leading to the emergence of a range of themes for associations. These are predominantly a product of associations working as the providers of new social housing; a role that is being undertaken in a more competitive marketplace, where there has been a reduction in state subsidies since 1992-93 and where access to non-governmental resources has become more important. The themes to emerge from this transformation include:

- diversification into regeneration and community facilities;
- diversification into care and special needs;
- diversification into private renting and contract management;
- the adoption of new organisational forms through mergers and group structures;
- a greater emphasis on a business ethos and management, and a changing regulatory regime to cope with the transformations (see below).

Pressures for change: environmental turbulence

The pressures that have led to the sector changing in nature, scale and scope, resulting in diversification, are not abating. Future pressures including household formation, economic restructuring and government policy proposals are set to ensure that associations have to remain alert to new challenges and innovation opportunities. Some aspects of this environmental turbulence are briefly considered:

- Household projections for England have anticipated major increases in the number of households (DoE, 1996; Holmans, 1997; DETR, 1999). Though the majority of these new households are expected to be housed in the private sector there will be a range of spillover effects for housing associations. These global projections also hide a widely different regional picture. A broad north—south split has been identified, with the south of England experiencing continued housing need and pressures for new social housing, while the north undergoes slower rates of household formation and a reduction in the demand for social housing.

- The overall economic picture is healthy with incomes rising and unemployment falling. This growing affluence has underpinned the general trend towards owner-occupation. However, two underlying features of this trend raise issues for housing associations, which were initially brought to our attention in the 1990s (Ford and Wilcox, 1994). First, employment is increasingly being dominated by fixed-term and temporary contracts that add uncertainty to people's housing careers and may necessitate new forms of renting or ownership. Second, while incomes continue to rise, those on the lowest incomes continue to see their income grow at a slower rate and associations will have to ensure that they are able to offer good quality affordable housing to those with least resources.

- Societal perceptions of the social rented sector have altered and have resulted in associated changes to patterns of its use. The sector is now the tenure of last resort for many of those it houses. This has contributed towards a self-perpetuating circle whereby perceptions of the product and its services are low. In particular, younger households are using the sector as a stepping-stone before entering owner-occupation (Cole et al, 1999) and as a temporary tenure, reducing the average length of tenancy, though clearly signalling the sector's future role.

- In addition to the external environment changing, the policy environment is set to be revolutionised. Housing associations are likely to form the main type of social housing provision by the end of the decade (DETR, 2000). Associations are expected to play central roles in regeneration and social exclusion, working in partnership with a range of organisations and developing new skills of neighbourhood management (SEU, 2000). Critically there are proposals emerging that will further limit rent rises which are currently pegged at the Retail Price Index plus 1%. The proposals to reduce this rate further and devise new methods to calculate rents are likely to have an impact on associations' financial and wider plans. They are predicted to affect the financial viability of some associations, notably those who have transferred from the local authority sector and are deeply indebted.

There are a multitude of influences and pressures for change which associations are experiencing and are going to have to manage in the short term. In some areas there will be a need to respond to ongoing pressures in other new challenges where associations will need to reconsider their purpose and the products they offer. What is certain is that this turbulence is unlikely to diminish.

Regulation and innovation in the housing association sector

Regulation has been a growing aspect of public services management since the mid-1990s and the 'audit explosion' (Power, 1998). Indeed some commentators argue that regulation is growing rapidly under Labour (Hood et al, 2000) while others have contended that central government has spun a 'myriad of little threads' around organisations that are responsible for service delivery (Hoggett, 1996, p 23). The housing association regulatory framework has recently been redesigned and bolstered to respond to specific issues in the sector and to reflect these wider regulatory processes. Our concern here is with the nature of regulation and its relationship to innovation.

The regulatory process is usefully explained by Hood et al (1999) who draw upon a cybernetic (control theory) perspective. They argue that regulation is concerned with:

- setting standards, or *directing*,
- gathering information about whatever is being controlled, or *detecting*, and
- modifying or changing behaviour, or *effecting change*.

This approach can be usefully applied to housing associations. First, they have to meet basic standards to be registered. Once in receipt of public funds they have to conform to Performance Standards (Housing Corporation, 1998b) which requires them to meet key standards in internal organisational governance, financial probity and the management of social rented housing. The Housing Corporation has at its disposal some of the most extensive detection mechanisms of any public services regulator (as shown by comparative research on public services regulation in Wales by Ashworth et al, 1999). This includes inspection, annual reports and plans, data and performance indicators, and budgetary controls. These detection devices are accompanied by extensive powers of intervention by the Corporation. Where associations run into 'difficulties' the Corporation has powers to change board members, to alter staffing and to 'shut down' associations. The Housing Corporation can also change the behaviour of associations in a number of other ways. This includes the development of policy to create new standards; a clear recent example of this is through their intervention on rents and rent setting. Part of its armoury of change mechanisms is its promotion of good practice and innovation through a programme of demonstration projects and the dissemination of good practice.

The extent of housing association regulation

Housing association regulation serves a number of purposes. Table 2 summarises these and highlights the predominantly social nature of housing association regulation, seeking to establish housing standards and the fair treatment of tenants within a framework for housing those in greatest need. The Housing Corporation (which is regulator and funder) has undertaken this role through audit, inspections and statistical returns since the establishment of its regulatory role in 1974. Regulatory activity has become more focused following the 1988 Housing Act and the large-scale introduction of mortgage lenders in the sector and the use of private finance. More recently the regulatory emphasis has moved away from a blanket approach, which sought to capture all associations, to one based on risk assessments. This seeks to identify those associations that may be at the greatest risk, that is those in receipt of large amounts of public subsidy or experiencing management difficulties. This shifting emphasis has been accompanied by an intensification of information requirements, for example the quarterly return of accounts.

Recently the Housing Corporation has extended its remit to the second form of regulation: economic. It now controls the costs of social housing to tenants. This represents a reversal in policy from the early 1990s when its attitudes towards rents were very much laissez-faire, reflecting those of the then Conservative administration. Building on a model developed by the Welsh regulator (see Walker and Smith, 1999 for an account), the Housing Corporation has imposed a rent

Table 2: The purpose and function of housing association regulation

Purposes	Description
Accountability for public resources	To ensure the economic, efficient and effective use of resources
Meeting social policy objectives	To use the regulatory regime to impose national policies, such as access to housing, tenant participation and so on
Good stewardship	To guarantee that associations provide adequate standards of management and service provision to tenants
Protection of housing association interests	Housing associations have used the regime to protect themselves from external pressures through the system of registration and the activities of the trade body
Comfort to private lenders	The regulatory regime is able to offer comfort to lenders, reducing the risks of their £14 billion investment in the sector
Responding to the needs of consumers	The regime ensures that consumers' needs are responded to and that they are able to influence and join the decision-making process, through complaints to involvement in organisational decision making

Source: Adapted from Day and Klein (1993); Mullins (1997b)

regime which only allows associations to increase rents by a maximum of the Retail Price Index plus 1%. The penalties for exceeding this can lead to a withdrawal of new public subsidy (made possible by the regulator-funder position). However, as public subsidy has substantially fallen, potentially weakening its position, the Corporation has turned to tactics such as 'naming and shaming' those whose rent increases exceed the target (Cooke, 1999). Current proposals continue this approach as government outlines plans to maintain affordable rents while retaining control over associations, some of whom are shifting their strategies to become financially independent organisations, though with large current and historic investments of public subsidy.

The extent and complexity of housing association regulation is witnessed in the range of other organisations that have an interest in their affairs. The constitution of an association leads to its regulation by one or more of Companies House or the Registrar of Friendly Societies or the Charities Commission. This can place additional constraints on associations; for example there have been ongoing debates about the definition of 'necessitous circumstances' for housing associations registered as charities. The scope of the sector and the movement by some associations into new areas of activity also exposes them to new areas and types of regulation. Thus associations providing personal social care services will also be inspected by their local authority social services department, placing a further set of externally imposed standards upon them. The 1996 Housing Act extended the Audit Commission's remit beyond local government and the health service to include advice on value-for-money measures and practices which housing associations could adopt. This has led to a number of studies which re-emphasise core business processes (for example Audit Commission/Housing Corporation, 1995, 1996a, 1996b, 1998). Furthermore, private financiers impose a range of internal controls on associations through the use of covenants and their expectations of organisational and financial management.

The regulation innovation interface

Intuitively innovation and regulation are diametrically opposed. The extent of the housing association regulation described above suggests that they are bound and constrained by the regime they have to work within: it is mechanistic, full of checks and balances, rather than organic and fluid. However, evidence exists from other fields to suggest that regulation is not necessarily constraining (Ramswamy et al, 1994). Nonetheless, the regulator-funder status of the Housing Corporation gives it a full set of regulatory tools to control the core business of social rented housing and all aspects of corporate governance and financial management (Housing Corporation, 1998b). Notwithstanding this the industry regulator argues that it promotes new ideas and acts as the agent which disseminates ideas across the sector positively to effect change and raise standards, through, for example, its Innovation and Good Practice Grants (Housing Corporation, 1998b). It is possible to suggest that the regulator is receptive to innovation, promoting it as 'good for the sector'. Alternatively innovation is perceived as a risky process, its impact cannot always be anticipated, and regulation seeks to ensure that the organisation or its users are not adversely affected – innovation can have negative as well as positive impacts.

These tensions are usefully illustrated by the debate led by the Housing Corporation (2000) during 1999 and 2000. At the heart of this has been the idea of regulating or containing diversity by limiting the proportion of non-core activities an association can undertake. This ensures that where associations move into new markets and/or develop new services, their activity falls within the Housing Corporation's regulatory regime. This has led to a new, wider definition of social rented housing:

> ... homes for letting or low-cost homeownership and associated amenities and services for people whose personal circumstances make it difficult for them to meet their housing needs in the open market. [It] ... covers schemes for workers in key public services; PFI schemes involving ownership and management; community regeneration initiatives; residential care homes and low-cost homeownership schemes. The definition excludes market-rented schemes, student accommodation and some registered nursing homes. (Dow, 2000, pp 12-13)

The new regime specifies diversity by classifying an association's finances. An association with more than 5% of its turnover or capital in non-core activities is defined as a diversified organisation. This puts in place a range of reporting requirements, including self-certifying whether the association falls above or below this threshold; ensuring that diversified activity does not pose any risk to the social housing activity; notifying the Corporation of any indented non-core activity; and escalating supervision if non-core activity exceeds one third of total activities, while it must not exceed 49% to ensure that social housing is the main activity of a housing association.

The sectoral transformations stemming from the changed context within which associations now find themselves (highlighted earlier in the chapter), and the regulator's responses, do suggest that housing associations are capable of producing substantive change. The presentation of our findings later in the book will indicate the extent to which it is innovative or discontinuous or framebreaking. However, the regulator found it necessary to redesign its regime to accommodate changes introduced by associations. It is reasonable to argue that the changes introduced by regulatees are in part a product of regulatory regimes (even those as all-embracing as the Housing Corporation's) rather than the traditional assumption that it is competitive environments that are necessary for innovation. This is suggested because regulatory regimes and problems can create the capacity for innovation. For example, Mullins (1997b) highlights the process of regulatory capture, noting the substantial interplay between the staff of the regulator and of associations. This is seen as providing the regulator with specialist skills and knowledge about associations and means it can remain abreast of the key developments and issues in the sector. However, it can also mean that the capacity for independent judgement is clouded as the distance is reduced between the regulator and regulatee. Therefore there is a need to understand the 'extent' to which the regulatee/regulator closeness promotes change rather than innovation because closeness will allow the regulator to influence associations and prompt different courses of action. In addition, housing associations are part of the wider public sector and consequently there are problems of performance ambiguity. Consequently, it can be difficult to define appropriate standards, behaviour and outcomes – reflected by the regulator's more tangible focus on the property aspects and core business processes. The regulatory regime by its nature involves regulators intervening to rectify past problems. Therefore, it can be difficult to detect the activities of associations and thus effect the 'right' change by the regulator when there are problems of performance ambiguity. This then gives associations space for innovation – what is a problem or a failure for the regulator may be an innovation for an association. More simply, the barrier cast by the regulatory regime provides associations with a clear line of 'acceptable' and 'non-acceptable' behaviour. It is relatively easy for an association to see an innovation opportunity because there is a clear line in front of them. The challenge is ensuring that the innovations are acceptable to the regulator or developed without the regime. Following the changes to the Housing Corporation's regime and its relatively recent move into economic regulation, a form of regulation seen to result in innovation in many other sectors such as, notably, the privatised utilities, the question remains to what extent it will constrain or liberate the innovative housing association.

This discussion suggests that the areas for innovation or framebreaking present themselves at the boundaries of association activity and regulatory competence. Innovation and regulation are simultaneously concerned with effecting change. Regulatory change is concerned with meeting standards, including probity, collecting evidence for compliance or promoting new ways of delivering products and services with an emphasis upon control. As a funder-regulator and government agency the

Corporation can also effect change through its ability to make policy, for example the introduction of rent regulation, which has substantial impact on associations. Innovation is concerned with discontinuous change, often in reaction to 'shocks' (Schroeder et al, 1989) that may be effected by the organisation itself or from external action, including that of the regulator. Innovation is then concerned with new markets, groups of users or services. There are significant tensions between the two concepts and the ways they are played out in practice, and the forms of change that are being promoted which, it is suggested, further contribute towards the innovative capacity of housing associations.

Conclusions

The housing association sector has undergone a major transformation since it was initially promoted as the new provider of social rented housing, changing in both its nature and scope. It has expanded substantially, though current projections are for rapid expansion as a new breed of associations enters the sector: Large Scale Voluntary Transfers and Local Housing Companies. The housing association sector is likely to experience ongoing turbulence as new pressures continue to bear down on them leading or forcing them into new areas of activities; however, some of these will be from their own volition and not all pressed upon them. These primarily external pressures, coupled with the expectations of the regulator, are hypothesised as the drivers of change and hence innovation in the sector. Indeed, these pressures have already led to the rapid diversification of housing association activity. Central to the innovation impacts of this turbulence and change is the nature of the regulatory regime and the extent to which this spurs associations to innovate or constrains their actions.

FOUR

Classifying and measuring innovation

This chapter demonstrates that housing associations have innovative capacity and identifies the types of innovation developed by the case-study associations, from stage one of the research. Having established that associations have innovative capacity we go on to examine innovation in the sector. This involves a methodological discussion about bibliographic sources and their use in public services management and public policy, and the role they can play in the development of 'evidence-based policy and practice'. The value of these techniques is shown and we make some preliminary comments on the nature of innovation in the housing association sector. By providing examples of innovation in individual associations and in the sector we provide 'benchmarks'. These can be updated on a continual basis to give associations a reliable standard of innovation within the sector. It can also be developed in other public services areas to enhance innovation knowledge and broaden benchmarks. Limitations to these techniques are noted, particularly the normative environment surrounding innovation and the capacity of associations for self-reporting innovation.

Innovation in housing associations: evidence from the stage-one case-studies

One of the main issues to emerge from the research was the internal focus of many innovations and the emphasis upon service innovations. Where total innovations were observed they related to some of the transformations seen at the sector level that were emerging during the late 1990s. This partly concurs with work on changing organisational direction by Mullins (1997a) though it identifies fewer examples of inter-organisational innovations than the work of Reid (1995). Six areas of innovative activity are discussed below.

Cultural change

This was a theme running through all the case-study associations. The pressures for cultural change were connected to the need to develop a 'business focus' – two of the associations commented they were seeking to achieve 'reduced costs and better quality services'. This reflected the growing financial pressures on the sector as a whole. For the East Dorset Housing Association, its transfer from council ownership into the housing association sector had exposed it to a new, more competitive environment where business focus became more important. In all cases financial pressures flowed from the private finance environment which meant that it was necessary to ensure income was collected and the stock was of a good condition both to repay existing loans and attract new ones. Alongside the performance measures set by private lenders to achieve this, the regulator now requires, as was noted above, a more sophisticated range of performance and management information. These pressures were reflected in each association where different forms of performance measurement and staff appraisal systems had been put in place. The relationship between organisational performance and staff rewards was seen most clearly at Riverside Housing Association, which had introduced a form of performance-related pay linked to key organisational objectives to reinforce the behaviour it wished to see among its staff. Each association had made moves towards staff empowerment to ensure that decisions were taken as close to the customer as possible to increase responsiveness, thereby reducing bureaucracy. A distinct aspect of each association's cultural change programmes was in summary to develop a more 'private sector ethos', shifting their position away from public and voluntary cultures, indicating their capacity to present themselves in different ways.

Customer focus/information technology

Customer focus and information technologies were used in conjunction to increase the responsiveness of services. Specific projects were undertaken to gain more detailed feedback from customers, including the use of questionnaire surveys and focus groups, the results of which were subsequently used to inform management decisions. For example, East Dorset built on the statutory consultation required with tenants before the stock transfer. This interaction with tenants led to an ongoing process of consultation and data collection, typically through the use of consultants. The constitutional structure has also led to the appointment of tenant members to the board. The emphasis on customer focus has been pressed by the regulator, keen to encourage greater organisational accountability to tenants, and has been central to their interpretation of Best Value (Housing Corporation, 1998c).

The move to more responsive services was seen at Riverside and Touchstone Housing Association through the development of call centres, as a new form of service delivery. This adopted innovation from banking and insurance services was seen to be much more responsive to tenants than traditional methods of communication. Call centres represent a substantial change in the delivery of services to customers by focusing the predominantly administrative aspects of the housing management service into one point of contact, a telephone operator. They also represent new ways of working, as operatives become multiskilled dealing with the range of housing management services. The introduction of call centres led to the development of other areas of information technology to manage knowledge. This includes the more frequent use of e-mail, document imaging and the development of intranets. The generic and remote nature of call centre service delivery means that the associations are in turn able to market their services to other associations and their tenants.

Diversification

Expansion was achieved through the diversification of provision. Two key examples of this were identified: private sector renting and housing plus. Private sector renting (renting homes on the open market at a market rent) was developed to provide a wider asset base for two of the associations, to house a different user group, and to generate profits for the social side of the business. It also allowed associations to become established in new areas where they could subsequently become involved in their more mainstream social housing activities, as a legitimate local provider. Housing plus is the provision of a range of individual and community services beyond traditional property-based housing management, examples of which include furnished tenancies, community centres, youth schemes, and so on. It was used by one association to ensure it accesses new development opportunities, as well as delivering new services to existing tenants, while another developed community services for existing users.

New management techniques

New typically private sector management techniques were adopted in each association, often as tools to manage change. Touchstone had a long pedigree in the use of these techniques. Its current chief executive joined the association from the private sector in the 1970s and applied production management and manufacturing techniques to the rehabilitation of homes to increase their output above that of other associations, which would be competing for public subsidy. The use of private sector techniques continued in the association. It introduced a version of Total Quality Management (TQM) in the late 1980s and has more recently used business-process re-engineering (BPR) techniques. Process-based benchmarking visits, typically to non-housing organisations, were used by Riverside to examine teamwork and information technology.

Management techniques were introduced to achieve organisational goals, adopting the hard and soft technologies of new public management, to ensure a wider ownership of organisational goals through vision statements, as noted in the discussion of cultural change above. Many new management techniques were used also to implement innovations, including project management and BPR. In essence these were deployed in the form of new-product development teams to develop new ideas for service delivery, new products or the ideas of executives.

Organisational expansion

Organisational or stock expansion was a common theme in all associations. The two 'traditionally' structured associations (see below) have continued to expand through their development programmes and through partnerships and have benefited from the new financial regime. However, the funding difficulties faced by the sector from 1993 onwards, together with business and financial pressures, have led to an increase in the number of mergers. Touchstone was a product of a merger while another, Riverside, merged with an association during the research, taking it into its devolved structure. The perceived dynamism and innovative capacity which growth brings led one of the associations explicitly to seek geographical growth, though this also overcame the problems of low investment where the majority of its stock was located.

Organisational structure

Of the associations, East Dorset has a relatively traditional housing association structure of one registered company with a single office. Touchstone has a number of regional offices and a range of linked companies. Both of these organisations attempt to deliver a standard housing management product to tenants. Riverside, however, has developed a core and periphery organisational structure through the establishment of divisions, each with its own board that has authority delegated from the main board. The aim here has been to achieve more locally appropriate decision making, developing local policy and procedure, and to allow for geographical growth.

Categorising the housing associations' innovations

Having described, and given some context to the innovations identified by the associations, Figure 3 provides the primary classification against Osborne's typology. As was noted above, the emphasis has been upon internal innovations to improve processes. This is typically seen as a sign of more mature organisations that are seeking to improve efficiency, rather than to develop new products. The evidence here suggests that the case-study associations are predominantly 'mature' organisations (having existed in one form or another for many years) focusing upon service innovations to improve efficiency and performance. For example, innovations have been seen by existing tenants as the operations of the organisation's change to provide new or highly adapted services. This is clearly seen in the case of call centres which extend the use of telephone-based working, but are new services because of the adoption of this way of working as 'normal'. Organisational expansion seeks to provide the association's existing services to new groups of users (for example ex-council tenants or tenants of another association) or existing services to different users (for example through geographical growth) and are expansionary activities. New management techniques and cultural change do not sit neatly within Osborne's typology as they are processes which seek to enhance organisational performance (that is improve or introduce new services) but are neither a new service nor meet new users' needs. They have been classified as developmental innovations because of this, with a clear focus on continuous improvement. However, they have the capacity to facilitate innovation, to introduce new services (for example the call centre in one association emerged from its use of

Figure 3: The case-study housing associations' innovations classified

USERS

		New	**Existing**
SERVICES	**New**	*Total innovations* Diversification (eg private renting, housing plus) Customer focus (eg call centres)	*Evolutionary* Organisational structures (eg network form)
	Existing	*Expansionary* Organisational expansion (eg stock transfers, mergers)	*Developmental* New management techniques (eg TQM, BPR) Cultural change (eg business focus)

BPR) and to manage the innovation implementation process. The total innovations associated with diversification were seen towards the end of our research period as the associations came to terms with their changed world and developed new services for both new and existing tenants.

The secondary classification is based upon key attributes identified as influencing innovation in other research (Wolfe, 1994). Two examples are discussed for illustrative purposes – call centres and private renting – and are shown in Table 3. Call centres are technological innovations and part of the basic work activity of an association; radical because they introduce new behaviour; central because they affect the majority day-to-day workings of the organisation; flexible because they can be modified to the needs of an association; low on uncertainty because it is not a new information and communication technology; and, highly pervasive as they affect the majority of the organisation. Its centrality, adaptability and low uncertainty affirm the argument that the regulator does not find this innovation high risk or a threat to the regulatory regime. Its radicalness is not seen as problematic because it forms part of the regulator's key competencies. The regulator was able to gain control over the new process through its sponsorship of good practice and demonstration projects (Coopers & Lybrand, no date). By contrast the private renting classification is diametrically opposed and can therefore be seen to present itself to the regulator as a very different form of innovation. It involves new markets and services and is a more risky venture than developing a call centre. It is more uncertain as successful outcomes are not guaranteed and though its centrality is low, not concerning the major day-to-day work of the organisation, the financial investment and the potential impact of a problem on an association's performance and balance books are high. These factors are compounded by its inflexibility.

This second-stage analysis indicates the relevance of Wolfe's six attributes to this study of housing association innovation. However, a central facet of this study is omitted in other research. Risk has not been highlighted as significant. This may be because there are no other public services studies of innovation and regulation or because the use of private finance is more extensive among housing associations than other public services sectors. The discussion here and in Chapter 3 has highlighted the importance of risk on a number of occasions. The addition of risk (defined as the level of risk or liability to which an adopting organisation is exposed [Meyer and Goes, 1988]) to the list of secondary attributes aids the study of housing association innovation and innovation in other public services. In relation to the two innovations discussed here this variable would suggest that call centres were low risk and private renting high risk.

This additional classification stage of our work has captured the complex nature of innovations and their attributes. It has also indicated that clear innovation classification is necessary because of the contingent nature of innovation.

Table 3: Secondary innovation classification of call centres and private renting

Attributes	Call centre	Private renting
Organisational focus	Technological	Administrative
Radicalness	High	Low
Centrality	Central	Peripheral
Adaptability	Flexible	Inflexible
Uncertainty	Low	High
Pervasiveness	High	Low
Risk	Low	High

Measuring the extent of innovation in the housing association sector

Having established that housing associations have innovative capacity, the authors now go on to examine the potential use of the Literature-Based Innovation Output Indicator (LBIOI) to measure innovation. This technique uses bibliographic sources to describe the nature and extent of innovation. We demonstrate that this technique is of use in the housing association sector and can play a wider role in public policy and management to develop evidence-based policy and practice.

The Literature-Based Innovation Output Indicator

The promotion of innovation is a relatively new phenomenon for public services organisations. This means that there is no defined or generally accepted measurement approach. Public services innovation authors (for example Osborne, 1998) have used techniques developed in the 1960s and 1970s, such as Aston Measures. However, these are measures of the structural characteristics of innovative organisations, a theme of research in its own right, rather than methods to discuss the characteristics of a sector. We have therefore turned to the private sector literature and models. A number of problems have been identified with existing measures in the private sector. First, measures of Research and Development activity indicate levels of input into the innovation development process, not outputs. Furthermore, there is no tradition of large-scale Research and Development in many public services sectors. Second, patents represent inventiveness or creativity and not innovation. They are also highly product-focused and discretionary – innovations might not be patented. Third, surveys have been the more traditional approach in assessing the innovativeness of firms or the rate of adoption of innovations (Chapter 2). However, questionnaire surveys have their own methodological problems and are a burden to organisations. Literature-based innovation output indicators have been developed in response to these problems. Coombs et al (1996) in their application of this technique in the UK private sector use technical journals as their information source and to classify the innovations. Their classified innovations are then descriptively compared to standard innovation research variables such as innovation origin. The technique therefore moves away from inputs, measures of creativity and difficulties associated with questionnaire surveys.

However, the use of LBIOI raises a number of issues for public services research. Though technical journals are plentiful there is no tradition of carrying 'new product announcements' as there is in the private sector. Second, social policy innovations are likely to be both product and process and the technique has previously been prone to capture only product innovations (Coombs et al, 1996). Third, the reporting of innovations in 'technical' or professional public sector journals is not necessarily independently controlled by an editor as it is for private sector journals. It is therefore reliant upon the reporting of innovation, which could reflect the self-marketing capacities of organisations and the political necessity of being seen to be innovating. Notwithstanding these variations from the private sector model, data sources exist for innovation announcements in the public services. In particular the growth of good practice, often validated by professional agencies, regulators or government departments, is an important development and source of information in addition to professional journals.

The model has a number of strengths. The method does not burden public services organisations, unlike direct surveys. It does not rely upon 'snap-shot' or one-off surveys because it is a continuous approach, building longitudinal data sets. The methodology can be comparative, between different public services and different countries. A number of weaknesses are also found in the model. These include the problems of judgement over journal content. The possibility that some public services organisations will be better at generating announcements of their innovations than others or accessing funding opportunities for innovative work also needs to be borne in mind. In current (private sector) usage the model has been biased towards product and does not capture process innovations particularly well. However, by developing the breadth of the literature sources and adopting Osborne's broader typology of innovation classification, this problem can be addressed.

In summary, though a number of weaknesses have been suggested, the method has a number of key uses:

- it can be used to track innovation over time in the public services or in individual sectors.
- it can be used to track innovation adoption and diffusion rates, again across all public services or between them.
- with the range of data that is available on the performance of many public services organisations, and in particular in the quality of measures in the housing association sector, it would be possible to explore the consequences of innovation (Damanpour, 1991). This

would mean that the relationship between innovation and performance, in the longer term, could be examined and the impact of government policies assessed.

• these benefits have to be placed against the problems of working with self-reported data, a product of the normative climate surrounding innovation.

These factors suggest it is both a useful and important technique and would provide very important sources of information to develop more evidence-based policy and practice. We now go on to outline the data sources and information for our exploratory application of the LBIOI and present results.

Information collected for the database

Data were collected for the period 1997-99 for all English housing associations. The data sources used were readily identifiable as the professional housing press (*Agenda, Housing, Housing Today, Inside Housing*). In addition to these publications, data were collected from the Housing Corporation's Innovation and Good Practice Database. This contained 817 entries. The Housing Corporation's database contains information on innovation, good practice, research projects and dissemination activities. Housing associations in this database were undertaking projects supported by the regulator as part of its role to support innovation. The projects included were unlikely to develop without external support because they involved new activity or dissemination which is not a core housing association function. They had to produce results which could be generalised or diffused across the sector. Consequently, innovations had to be identified against stage one of our innovation classification system (it was not possible to undertake stage two, as this required more detailed knowledge than was available). Where insufficient information was available about either the innovation or the housing association the information was ignored. This led to a total database of 257 innovations in English housing associations. This was made up of 186 from the Housing Corporation database and 71 from publications.

The information collected broadly followed Coombs et al's (1996) approach. Information was collected on the following issues:

Innovation description: the innovation was briefly described.

Housing association identity: the housing association responsible for bringing the innovation to the sector was identified and its name recorded.

Type of innovation: the innovation was classified against Osborne's typology. This part of the research is dependent upon the judgement of the individuals who are creating the database. To ensure consistency the research team independently classified the innovations and then compared their results. Discrepancies were discussed until a consensus was reached after reclassification (Coombs et al, 1996).

Origin of the innovation: information about the national identity of the innovation was collected because context plays an important role in social policy innovations. For example, past policy importation has failed due to a lack of understanding of context (see Clapham and Kintrea, 1987).

Partnership innovation: the research by Coombs et al (1996) on the private sector noted that 'novel', or in our nomenclature total innovations, were more likely to be found in joint ventures. In the housing association sector we have seen an emphasis upon inter-organisational working and the emergence of a range of new inter-organisational practices (Reid, 1999).

Location of the innovation: the location of the innovation was noted to see if there were any geographical trends with some regions expressing a higher level of innovation.

Findings

We explore the data to see if the technique provides useful findings on the nature of innovation in the housing association sector. Chapter 5 goes on to provide more detailed research to explain the characteristics of innovative organisations. The results are presented under the following headings: type of innovation; origin of innovation; and distribution of innovations across the housing association sector.

Table 4: Type of innovation

Innovation classification	Number of innovations	%
Total	16	6
Expansionary	31	12
Evolutionary	104	41
Developmental	106	41
All	257	100

Table 4 illustrates the range of innovation types using the Osborne typology. Nearly 60% of activities captured in our sample could be classified as major innovations – developing new services or serving new users. Of these the largest proportion developed services for existing users. A smaller proportion expanded their user base while 6% developed total innovations. Figure 3 (p 52) illustrates these types of innovation for our case-study associations and similar innovations were identified in the sector as a whole. An example of a total innovation was the movement of associations into private renting where they served different users and had to develop new services. Expansionary innovations were often associated with stock transfers and various kinds of both formal and informal alliances between associations. Evolutionary innovations were seen in the development of new community services to housing association tenants and development or incremental innovations focused upon organisational development and training. It would be expected that for any sector there would be more developmental activity than other types because such activity involves less risky developments that are based on known efficiency of both processes and products, and on known end users. It could also be argued that a public services organisation would be more likely to innovate to provide known end users with new products or processes rather than expand to provide new end users, given their nature and purpose.

The origin of the innovation, between domestic and international, is shown in Table 5. The table illustrates the dominance of the domestic context for these ideas, which can be explained by the relatively parochial nature of housing associations in the international sector. Table 6 indicates that nearly half the innovations were undertaken by a single housing association, rather than in partnership with other housing associations or other organisations. Partnerships were more likely to be with organisations other than housing associations, and included local authorities, consultants and a range of other private sector organisations.

Table 5: Geographical origin of innovation

Origin of innovation	Number of HAs	%
Domestic	250	97
International	7	3
Total	257	100

Table 6: Partnership origin of innovation

Partnership origin	Number of HAs	%
One HA alone	121	47
Partnership with other HAs	54	21
Partnership with other organisations	77	30
Total	257	100

Table 7: Distribution of innovations by region

Region	Number of reported innovations	%	Number of HAs in region	Innovation index
North	33	13	37	0.89
North West	37	15	57	0.65
West Midlands	34	14	37	0.92
Eastern	16	6	49	0.33
South West	15	6	31	0.48
South East	34	14	54	0.63
London	82	33	88	0.93

There is an uneven spread of reported innovations; in particular, nearly one third of all those reported were based in London (Table 7). This may be partly explained by the greater number of associations in the region. The innovation index in Table 7 reveals that while London remains the most innovative region, the propensity to innovate is high in both the North and West Midlands regions.

Table 8: Innovation type by partnership arrangements

Classification of innovation	One HA alone %	Partnership with other HAs %	Partnership with other organisations %
Total	8.2	5.6	3.8
Expansionary	7.4	20.4	14.1
Evolutionary	37.7	35.2	48.7
Developmental	46.7	38.9	33.3
ALL	100.0	100.0	100.0

Chi² = 10.434; *p* = 0.081

We now go on to tabulate partnership and region against the type of innovation. The limited number of international originated innovations makes any inferences from Table 6 limited. That the international origins may have produced a number of total innovations disproportionate to what may have been expected seems intuitively reasonable, but the numbers are too small to make any strong inferences. Table 8 indicates that the total innovations were disproportionately sole rather than partnership activity, although the expansionary, and to a lesser extent, evolutionary innovations were disproportionately partnership activities (with other housing associations and non-housing associations respectively). The developmental activities were also disproportionately sole activities rather than in partnership with non-housing associations. These findings therefore lend some support to the Coombs et al study, and where it differs, in the case of total innovations, the numbers are relatively small. However, the results are not statistically significant. Table 9 illustrates the regional variations in the types of innovative activity, but is not significant. The South West regions produce disproportionately more total and expansionary innovations than might be expected.

The main feature of the results presented above is the emphasis by housing associations upon evolutionary innovation or developmental activity to provide services to existing user groups. Total innovation is limited in the housing association sector. However, this finding concurs with Coombs et al's (1996) work on private sector organisations (which suggests that 8% of reported innovation approximate to 'total' innovations) and Osborne's (1998) work on the personal social services.

Table 9: Innovation type by region

	Total %	Classification of innovation			
		Expansionary %	Evolutionary %	Developmental %	ALL %
North	6.0	6.0	42.4	45.4	100
North West	0	13.2	42.1	44.7	100
West Midlands	5.9	11.8	38.2	44.1	100
Eastern	6.2	25	37.5	31.3	100
South West	12.5	18.8	31.3	37.5	100
South East	2.9	8.8	47.1	41.2	100
London	9.8	11.6	39.5	39.5	100

$Chi^2 = 21.516$, $p = 0.608$

Conclusions

It has been clearly shown that housing associations produce a range of innovation and have an innovative capacity not dissimilar to that of other sectors. The classification of the innovations described in the chapter also indicates that associations develop total innovations in addition to incremental developmental innovations. The developmental innovations are clearly used in the process of managing innovation, either to produce new ideas (business–process re-engineering) or to manage the innovation process (project management). However, by adopting a second level of innovation classification we were able to illustrate graphically that the nature of total innovations can vary. The examples of call centres and private rented housing showed how total innovations, which would be expected to require the development of a range of new management skills because they involve a break with the past, can be differently assessed. This careful specification of innovation aids not only researchers when considering their analysis and findings but also managers when determining the organisational and management requirements to put new working practices into place.

The second half of this chapter explored the LBIOI methodology. It has indicated that it can play an important role in public services research and management. It has been adapted to the public services sector by adopting Osborne's innovation typology. This provides a clearer picture of non–product-based innovation and enhances the classification system adopted by Coombs et al (1996) in their private sector study. Its usefulness as a research methodology and tool has been illustrated in our study of housing associations where new findings have been presented on innovation in the sector. This suggests that the technique 'captures' data that have some validity and reliability and gives an explanation of the nature, location and extent of innovation in a public services sector.

There are, however, a number of methodological issues that need to be recognised. In particular, the sources of literature used in studies would need to be fully described to ensure clarity about the use of reported innovations and to recognise the conspicuous use of innovation by public services organisations. Furthermore, this approach is not a substitute for primary research data on public services innovation – it can complement or supplement them – to provide modest databases. However, at a time when public services organisations are ever increasingly researched, bibliographic techniques provide an alternative approach to data collection to build pictures of innovation activity in sectors. Critically, its main advantage is that it does not burden organisations with questionnaire completion, being a technique to describe the nature of innovation in a sector, and not just to describe the innovations.

Bearing these issues in mind the approach could usefully be extended. Longitudinal studies of innovation could be undertaken to make comparisons between different sectors. The establishment of such data sets would also make it possible to begin to explore the relationship between innovation and performance in public services organisations and to track changes in the nature of innovations developed by public services organisations and the context within which they work. This would aid government and public services managers in their decision making and wider public services innovation research.

FIVE

In search of the innovative housing association

Housing associations have developed a range of innovations. Over recent years these innovations have placed emphases upon services to existing users and ongoing incremental innovations, or continuous improvements to services in keeping with government public services programmes, such as Best Value. In this chapter we move on to explore the characteristics of innovative housing associations and seek to answer a number of questions. These include:

- Are the innovative associations small or large?
- Do they have many or only a few staff?
- How extensive are their operations?
- What is their geographical spread?
- Are there staff specialists?
- Have they appointed new senior managers recently or has their senior management team been static?

The answers to these questions will allow associations to rank themselves against our population of innovative associations, and compare themselves to the innovative characteristics and the archetypal innovative association presented in the conclusion to this chapter. The explanations of the innovative housing association we offer relate to the people or actors in the association, the nature of the organisation and its management.

The database used in the chapter includes 474 housing associations. These vary in size, from around 100 homes in management to over 20,000. The housing associations included in the analysis are those that are developing and/or own 250 or more units. While these associations represent only about a quarter of the total number of registered housing associations, they constitute the population of 'active' housing associations (Chapter 3), that is housing associations who have a critical size (250 or more units) or who are actively developing regardless of size. This distinction is important, as it allows the analysis to ignore registered housing associations with no intention of being innovative because their aims are to manage and maintain their stock. Small almshouses would fall into this category. The analysis presented here does, nevertheless, offer useful lessons to smaller associations, in keeping with the findings in the last chapter which noted smaller associations' use of partnerships for innovation.

These 'active' associations in our study are also those that are regulated by the Housing Corporation. This is because they are either currently in receipt of, or have been the recipients of public subsidy. As part of the annual regulatory process these associations complete a detailed questionnaire that provides information on their staff, organisation, management, and so on: the Regulatory and Statistical Return (RSL) (Long). This questionnaire provides the data used in our analysis. This method, as with our approach in Chapter 4, does not burden organisations with questionnaire completion but relies upon secondary data sources. The number of housing association innovations presented here is slightly less than that discussed in relation to the Literature-Based Innovation Output Indicator discussed in Chapter 4. A number of the associations picked up in the literature searches in Chapter 4 do not complete the detailed regulatory questionnaire and no data was available on them, while one third of those identified as developing innovations within the sector were not registered housing associations (see Table 6). Thus our sample consists of 474 associations who complete the RSL (Long) of which 90 have reported 140 innovations. The dependent variable in our analysis is whether an association innovates or not, that is has it developed any one of a total, evolutionary, expansionary or developmental innovation. Our databases suggest that 19% of housing associations had developed and reported one of these four types of innovation.

The analysis of this data set has used two statistical techniques. First, the variables were considered in terms of the significant differences in the mean of innovating and non-innovating associations and significance tests of those differences (t-test). Second, they were analysed to investigate the extent to which there is a relationship between innovation and the variables. The correlation presented is the Tau-C test that allows all types of variable to be considered. Finally, we compared the variables used in the study through a multiple regression (a logistic Forward LR regression) to highlight those characteristics discussed which were the most significant in predicting which organisations were innovative.

Explaining organisational innovativeness

We focus upon three sets of independent variables to explain organisational innovativeness: the characteristics of the actors or people in the organisation and the way they are organised, the nature of the organisation and its management.

People explanations

Specialisation

Specialisation is explored through a breakdown of the staff composition. It includes the profile of staff, the staff mix and numbers of different types of staff in the core social housing categories of housing management, development, central services and administration, care services and other. These categories are important because they indicate different types of technical knowledge, which play an important role in innovation (Bigoness and Perreault, 1981). Specialists are important for innovation because they have different skills in different areas. A variety of skills enhances innovation because the specialists are able to share ideas, techniques and procedures. The merits of different specialist teams have long been debated in the social housing sector, for example, the debate between the development and housing management specialisations. It is assumed that a development team, which expands the organisation through the proactive development process (identifying new land and partners, and funding contractors) and searches for new markets and expansion opportunities, results in a more dynamic and hence innovative organisation. This reflects the housing association cries of 'develop or die' from the 1990s. By contrast the housing management function is portrayed as more staid because of its emphasis upon maintaining the organisation through the functions of lettings, repairs and estate management. However, this is rhetoric – no evidence has been collected to explore this assumption. Specialisation across the organisation is assumed to be positively related to innovation in housing associations.

Professionalism

The degree or level of professional staff in an organisation is argued to be conducive to innovation. This is because the professional knowledge of organisational members is high as a result of being educated and gaining wide experience. This leads to greater boundary–spanning activities and therefore greater exposure to new ideas, which come from participation in professional activities (Pierce and Delbecq, 1977). It is also seen to increase self–confidence and a desire to move forward, be that either to gain recognition from peers or enhance organisational performance (Damanpour, 1987).

Organisation explanations

Innovation research has a long tradition of debating organisational structure (Burns and Stalker, 1962) and still provides contested results (Berry, 1994). Particular organisational factors are associated with innovation, notably those that measure size.

Size

Some adoption literature argues that there is no relationship between organisational size and innovation adoption (Utterback, 1974) while others have noted its potential for having both a positive and negative effect on innovation (Berry, 1994). However, the majority of the evidence suggests that the larger the organisation the more likely it is to innovate (Aitken and Hage, 1971; Damanpour, 1991; Rogers, 1995). This is typically because large organisations are more diverse and have more complex facilities that provide them with greater opportunities for cross-fertilisation of ideas and a range of skills that facilitates innovation (for example Damanpour, 1987; Meyer and Goes, 1988; Rogers, 1995; Zaltman et al, 1973). It can also be hypothesised that larger organisations can absorb the costs of innovation, and abortive projects. Our measure of size is the number of units owned by an association. It is argued that size has a positive relationship to innovation.

Innovation often requires additional staff and resources for its development and implementation (Cyert and March, 1963). Wider evidence from the innovation literature also suggests that organisations with abundant staff are more likely to be innovators (Berry, 1994). The total number of different individuals, full-time equivalents (FTE), available to the organisation is an indication of the resources that are likely to be available to an association to undertake innovative activities. Our second size hypothesis also suggests a positive explanation of innovation: the more staff a housing association has the more likely it is to innovate.

Functional differentiation

Functional differentiation represents the extent to which an organisation undertakes different tasks and functions within separate parts of the organisation. Different skills and groups of staff who will be able to recognise and introduce innovations will be found in different parts of the organisation. For example, stronger marketing skills are likely to have been longer established with staff who provide low-cost homeownership schemes rather than other forms of housing. The management of different types of accommodation, thereby differentiating functions across the organisation, is a pervasive feature of public services housing organisations. This clearly serves to locate different tasks and functions in different parts of the organisation. We have hypothesised that the more units owned of a particular type, the greater the degree of differentiation into different departments. We would anticipate a positive relationship between innovation and functional differentiation (Damanpour, 1991).

Geographical spread

The number of local authority areas worked in is argued to be a further indicator of innovative organisational characteristics. Associations that operate in a large number of local authority areas are likely to be exposed to a greater range of organisations (Walker, 1994) from which ideas can be adopted. It is also an indication of the potential number of partner organisations a housing association could work with, a factor noted as relevant in relation to the nature of innovation in the housing association sector (Chapter 4). All aspects would suggest a positive relationship between the number of areas worked in and innovation.

Management explanations

Management team

The role and nature of the management team, and its stability or rate of turnover in an organisation, raise issues about the characteristics of innovative organisations. For example, Damanpour (1991) argues that longevity of managers in their jobs is to be positively associated with innovation because through their experience it enables them to bring new ideas to the organisation and management process. The role of the management team can be related to particular stages in the innovation process. For example, different skills are needed to implement innovations and bring new ideas to an organisation. Therefore, others have suggested that new leaders play a critical role in fostering organisational change (for example Peters and Waterman, 1982; Kanter, 1983; Van de Ven et al, 1999). This line of argument assumes that new managers may bring changes to an organisation to signal their own view of leadership, or to help implement their own priorities (Berry, 1994) that can act as triggers for innovation (Van de Ven et al, 1989). We argue that new leaders and managers are likely to increase the propensity of an organisation to innovate as they seek to stamp their new identity on the organisation. Our assessment of this variable for the associations in this study include the number of changes in management team staff and the ratio of change in management staff (number of changes over number of management staff).

Table 10 summarises the variables adopted to explain the characteristics of organisational innovativeness in housing associations, and defines the variables. The anticipated relationship of the variable to organisational innovativeness is positive in every case.

Table 10: The characteristics of innovative organisational variables

Variable	Definition
People	
Specialisation housing	Number of administrative, support, development, management and other staff working in the housing association
Professionalism	Number of professional members of the Chartered Institute of Housing
Organisation	
Size	Total units owned
	Total number of full-time equivalent (FTE) employed
Geographical spread	Number of local authority areas where an association owns stock
Functional differentiation	Number of different types of unit managed: general needs, market, supported and sheltered
Management	
Management team	Changes in senior staff and ratio of change among senior staff

The characteristics of innovative housing associations

Table 11 outlines the results of a comparison of mean scores and correlations for each of the factors associated with specialisation and professionalism. The differences between the mean score for four of the six variables were in the anticipated direction: innovative organisations are more professional than their non-innovating counterparts, though management and other non-housing staff were negative but insignificant. However, the level of professionalism was statistically significant at only the 95% confidence level for both tests, indicating a strong positive relationship explaining the characteristics of the innovative association. It indicates the exposure certain staff will have, for example to publications, and other individuals, through their professional membership, and therefore to new ideas. The findings indicate that professional membership has a significant relationship to innovation, with innovating associations having over three times as many professional staff as non-innovating ones.

Table 11: The people characteristics of innovative housing associations

Variable		Mean (t-test)	Tau-C
Specialisation			
Housing management staff	Innovative	53.85	−0.009
	Non-innovative	60.15	
Development staff	Innovative	8.38	0.042
	Non-innovative	5.77[b]	
Administrative staff	Innovative	18.92	0.048
	Non-innovative	16.92	
Care staff	Innovative	24.8	0.01
	Non-innovative	32.8	
Other non-housing staff	Innovative	10.33	−0.044
	Non-innovative	3.7	
Professionalism			
Number of professional staff	Innovative	17.16	0.34[a]
	Non-innovative	5.28[a]	

Notes: a Significant at the 95% interval (one-tailed); *b* Significant at the 90% interval (one-tailed)

Specialisation would not appear to be a significant explanation of innovation within associations. The existence of housing management, administrative, care and other staff shows no statistical significance. The only explanation that had a significantly different mean for the variables which demonstrate the level of specialisation was the number of development staff. Thus the presence of a development team indicates that some specialisation is important in characterising the innovative housing association. This provides some evidence to support the rhetoric of the early 1990s of 'develop or die' and the importance attached to this dynamic part of the organisation that keeps the organisation moving forwards.

The extent to which these variables correlate with each other, that is the extent to which there is a relationship between a variable and innovation, was insignificant for specialisation. However, the direction of the relationship for housing management staff and other non-housing staff was negative. This suggests that specialisation in these areas is antithetical, that is they hinder innovation.

Table 12: The organisational characteristics of innovative housing associations

Variable		Mean (t-test)	Tau-C
Size			
Total units owned	Innovative	5833.33	0.34[a]
	Non-innovative	1550.23[a]	
Total full-time equivalents	Innovative	120.23	0.018
	Non-innovative	130.50	
Functional differentiation			
General needs units	Innovative	4,882.97	0.32[a]
	Non-innovative	1,231.99[a]	
Units developed	Innovative	24.61	0.19[a]
without subsidy	Non-innovative	4.6[a]	
Supported units	Innovative	119.21	0.28
	Non-innovative	28.48[a]	
Sheltered units	Innovative	798.43	0.24[a]
	Non-innovative	234.32[a]	
Geographic Spread			
Number of local	Innovative	30.31	0.22[a]
authority areas	Non-innovative	10.99[a]	

Note: a Significant at the 95% interval (one-tailed)

Table 12 presents results for the organisational factors: size, functional differentiation and geographic spread. Each variable is significant at the 95% level for the comparisons of means and the extent of correlation bar, the second measure for size. All variables are in the predicted direction, that is all our variables positively explain innovation. There is support for the argument suggesting that organisational size is an important aspect of the innovative organisation with the larger housing association being more likely to innovate than the smaller one. This indicates the importance of housing associations possessing the capacity to dedicate resources to new projects in order to be innovative. Total units owned also has a high correlation confirming the importance attached to this explanation. Innovative associations are likely to own three times as much stock as non-innovating associations, with a stock-holding of nearly 6,000 homes. Total units owned is not, however, significant, thus the total number of full-time equivalent staff does not play a role in describing the innovative housing association.

We have suggested that functional differentiation, the extent to which an organisation is divided into different units or departments, has a significant positive relationship to innovation as the professionals within these units introduce more innovative practices (Damanpour, 1987). Our findings would again support this conclusion. The four types of differentiation measured are significant with the innovative housing association possessing a mixture of different tasks and functions within the organisation. The significance of this finding leads to further analysis. We explored the possible importance of providing either all four different mixes of tasks and functions or just two of those listed in Table 12. The results, all significant at the 95% confidence level, indicated that the innovative housing association provided nearly three (2.86) of the four mixes of tasks and functions in comparison to the non-innovative association which provided just over two (2.04). Therefore the innovative housing association would be expected to have a diversity of departments, tasks and functions, including the provision of market-based activities, and not to limit itself to one.

The number of local authority areas worked in is also significant in its findings, although the difference between innovators and non-innovators is not quite so substantial as for size (based on the correlation result). We argued that this aspect of organisational form enhances opportunities for developing partnerships. However, the broader range of activity may also be a factor in reducing the capacity to innovate and hence reducing the correlation coefficient.

Table 13: The management characteristics of innovative housing associations

Variable		Mean (t-test)	Tau-C
Management			
Change in senior staff	Innovative	0.70	−0.046
	Non-innovative	0.77	
Ratio of change	Innovative	0.39	0.008
	Non-innovative	0.38	

Table 13 shows that our two variables, change and the ratio of change in the management team, are not significant. We are therefore unable to confirm our explanation that innovative associations have a greater number of changes in staff, and have a greater ratio of change than do non-innovative ones. Nonetheless, the direction of the results do indicate a state of flux and change among the management team, supporting the notion that a change in senior management is a source of new ideas and hence innovation. The introduction of a new member to the management team could act as a catalyst for change, both in terms of a source of new ideas, and the power to implement them.

The results of the regression[1] are summarised in Table 14 (with more detail given in the footnote and Table 15). The table shows that five of our variables are significant and it confirms the importance of size. This variable provided the strongest explanation of innovative characteristics. Professionalism was again very significant. The results also reaffirm the importance of specialisation (which previously had been shown to effect innovation positively but not at a significant level) by highlighting particular groups of staff. Interestingly, support staff and development staff were important. It would appear that the provision of community care and care and support leads to innovative solutions to people's needs. It further confirms the significance of a development team. More startling is the confirmation of the relationship between housing management staff and innovation, as our findings here are again negative – a large housing management team is not conducive to innovation!

Table 14: The characteristics of innovative housing associations, summary regression results

Variable	R	Significance
Units owned	0.1128	0.0075
Support staff	0.0969	0.0160
Professional membership	0.0796	0.0326
Development staff	0.1358	0.0021
Housing management staff	−0.0812	0.0308

Note: all significant at 95% (see footnote for explanation of results)

The archetypal innovative housing association

We started this chapter by asking a number of questions about the characteristics of innovative housing associations. Our explanations and the predicted direction of these explanations received support from the statistical analysis. Our analysis suggests that the 'innovative housing association' has the following characteristics:

• it will be a larger association with nearly 6,000 units, if not more;
• it will have specialist staff, with support and development staff being particularly important, whereas a large number of housing management staff will reduce the capacity for innovation;
• it will have a high proportion of professional staff;
• it will work in nearly thirty different local authorities, if not more;
• it will have a variety of tasks and functions bringing together different skills and departments.

The strongest results have highlighted the importance of:

• organisational size, and
• the significance of specialised staff, particularly the development team, and professionals.

Size needs to be highlighted as a significant variable in explaining innovation. The impact of size suggests that it is not the small developing associations that are innovative, but the larger ones. Coupled with the evidence on development staff, this suggests that the innovative housing association will be 'active', expanding its range of activities and functions. Indeed, our description of the archetypal association looks like a 'regional' association.

Specialisation and professionalism are also significant findings. While many of these and other findings are broadly in line with the international research evidence, the significance of development staff is greater than many of the other variables. This relationship between development staff and innovation suggests that developmental activity is an important factor further explaining the propensity of housing associations to innovate. The ability of an organisation to expand and change itself, retaining organisational dynamism, is therefore critical and supports the intuitive arguments presented by associations over recent years. The findings do offer lessons to associations who might not fit the model of the 'regional' housing association – if they are involved in development activity they are more likely to be innovative. Similarly if they employ professionals they are more likely to be innovative.

Note

[1]The regression conducted was a logistic, Forward LR regression. A logistic multiple regression was used to explain what variables (characteristics) predict whether an organisation will be innovative or not. The dependent variable being predicted, therefore, was a dichotomous variable (0= no reported innovation, 1= reported innovation in the organisation).

The Forward LR method is a stepwise method that picks a series of variables (identified on the basis of a score criterion) and includes each one in turn, until no new variables affect the predictive power of the equation. The Forward LR method also examines the extent to which the selected variables impact on the equation if they are removed (using the likelihood ratio statistic). If the removal of the predictor makes a significant difference to how well the model predicts the data, the predictive variable is retained in the equation.

The findings (Table 15) are evaluated as being significant at the 95% confidence interval and the final model is correct 84.67%. The residuals were checked for outliers, and collinearity diagnostics were also analysed. There was significant multicollinearity (strong correlation between variables) with six of the variables; however, none of these variables proved significant in regression.

Table 15: The characteristics of innovative housing associations, regression results

Variables in the equation	B	SE	Wald	df	Sig	R	Exp (B)
Housing management	-0.007	0.0032	4.6665	1	0.0308	-0.0812	0.9930
Development staff	0.0572	0.0186	9.4687	1	0.0021	0.1358	1.0589
Units owned	0.0002	6.308E-05	7.1485	1	0.0075	0.1128	1.0002
Support staff	0.0034	0.0014	5.8003	1	0.0160	0.0969	1.0034
Professional membership	0.0451	0.0211	4.5658	1	0.0326	0.0796	1.0462
constant	-2.592	0.2441	112.7439	1	0.0000		

-2 Log likelihood: 311.648

Percentage correct: overall 84.67%[*]

Model if term removed

Term removed	-2 Log LR	df	Significance of Log LR
Housing management	6.419	1	0.0113
Development staff	10.281	1	0.0013
Units owned	7.364	1	0.0067
Support staff	7.644	1	0.0057
Professional membership	4.609	1	0.0318

Notes: [*] Not innovative was correct 96.82%, innovative was correct 30.77%

Key to Table 15

-2 Log LR	Indicates the amount of unexplained information. The larger the statistic, the greater the amount of unexplained information
Significance of Log LR	The significance of the log LR indicates the effect of removing the variable. If it is significant, then the variable should not be removed as it has a significant effect on the predictive value of the model
B	Coefficient of variable (represents the change in the logit (the natural log of the odds) of the outcome variable associated with a one-unit change in the predictor variable)
SE	Standard error: the standard deviation between sample means
Wald	Indicates whether B is significantly different from zero. If the difference is significant, then the predictor variable is making a significant contribution to the outcome
df	Degrees of freedom, the number of observations free to vary (n-1), in this case always 1
Significance	at the 95% confidence interval
R	Partial correlation between the outcome variable and the predictor. It varies from -1 to +1. A positive value indicates that as the predictor increases, so does the outcome, the value of the statistic indicates the amount of contribution this predictor makes
Exp (B)	Indicates the change in odds resulting from a unit change in the predictor. If the value is greater than 1 then, as the predictor increases, the odds of the outcome occurring increases

SIX

Managing innovation

Most people are clinging to the bank, afraid to let go and risk being carried along by the current of the river. At a certain point, each person must be willing simply to let go, and trust the river to carry him or her along safely. At this point he learns to 'go with the flow' and it feels wonderful.

Once he has gotten used to being in the flow of the river, he can begin to look ahead and guide his own course onward, deciding where the course looks best, steering his way around boulders and snags, and choosing which of the many channels and branches of the river he prefers to follow, all the while still 'going with the flow'. (Gawain, 1982 quoted in Quinn, 1988, p 164)

The way in which housing associations manage the rugged terrain of innovation will be explored in this chapter. The chapter is built around the experiences that our case-study associations have had on their innovation journey. These associations, from stage one of the research, provide our richest evidence of 'going with the flow' and their endeavours are drawn upon extensively and reported in the body of the text. The chapter also presents the stage-two case-study selected from the innovative associations discussed in Chapter 5. The sample for these associations was based upon a number of factors. The type of innovation (total, evolutionary, expansionary, developmental) was proportionately selected from within the database. A description of the innovation was examined to ensure that a variety of innovation examples were captured, including housing production as well as housing management ones. This resulted in the selection of fifteen stage-two cases, of which four did not proceed. The remaining eleven cases were undertaken through a mixture of telephone and face-to-face interviews and the analysis of documents. Illustrative examples of how six of these stage-two case-study organisations experienced their journey of managing the innovation process are highlighted at appropriate junctures in boxes.

The structure of the chapter follows the process theory framework presented in Chapter 2 (Van de Ven et al, 1989, 1999). We elaborate on the framework to illustrate the detailed aspects of each temporal period of initiation, development and implementation. Lessons on the management of innovation are drawn out and notable issues include the role of teams and teamwork, projects, pilots and experiments, and various forms of project management. These enabled the processes of innovation development and appropriation or implementation to be successfully managed through both 'deep' (experimentation prior to implementation, that is a pilot, demonstration project on trial in one part of the organisation) and 'broad' (rapid implementation across the whole organisation without experimentation) implementation strategies.

Initiating innovation

Organisation leaders (executives) in the associations were keen to challenge existing organisational practices, anticipate change and bring ideas from outside housing and the public services sector. This was neither simply the aspiration of leaders keen to promote their organisation nor the product of current management fads in respect of which every association was 'jumping on board'. For example, Coventry Churches Housing Association was adopting private sector management practices in the late 1970s when it applied manufacturing techniques to the rehabilitation of properties to increase output. Leaders were often labelled 'visionary' or 'dynamic' by their colleagues as they saw their organisations in a different light, achieving new possibilities. These visions were not just about creativity, but typically came from a range of tried and tested techniques to search out opportunities, identify the need for change and understand the changing nature of the environment within which their associations operated. This included boundary-scanning, which has become formalised over recent years and is now expected in the Best Value process through the use of generic benchmarking. There were frequent site visits to private sector firms such as Birmingham Midshires, Daf Layland, Pilkington, Tesco, and so on, to explore their approach to generic management processes, such as teamworking and approaches to knowledge management. Thinking about the applicability of management practices or projects from other sectors, through relatively simple tasks such as reading newspaper job advertisements for private sector positions, also contributed towards boundary-scanning activities. However, staff were not allowed to wander off on random searches for ideas that might one day solve a problem; rather they focused their activities. Search patterns that were too focused did not open up new opportunities or insights; a balance had to be struck. These search processes practically manifested themselves in 'away days' for the board and/or senior executives, regular policy review papers at board meetings when there were opportunities for reflective and strategic thinking or the use of consultants to bring in expert knowledge on an issue that was of interest or needed to be developed. These initiatives were sometimes supplemented by specialised management training. For example, some associations have used international visits or training and education at universities in different countries to broaden the experiences and expectations of their senior managers.

These activities, which might not initially appear related to specific innovations, were essential for innovation initiation and development. These periods of gestation would often provide a reservoir of ideas, knowledge and practices that could trigger the recognition of the need for change. They helped to generate knowledge about, for example, technological advances and what was technologically possible: thus two of our cases were at the vanguard of the development of call centres in the housing association sector, and the public services field. It also ensured that associations were "ahead of the game" (senior manager at Riverside), being proactive and seeking to alter the external environment, and the regulatory framework in particular, themselves rather than reacting to imposed change or edict. Thus one of our case-studies was one of a number of associations which pre-empted the marketisation project. Coventry Churches' activity as a speculative developer of homes for older people in the early 1980s gave it a reputation as a market leader. This in turn provided a stock of knowledge about working in a more market-led environment which has served it well in more recent times when diversification of funding opportunities, new, more cost-effective methods of development and more sophisticated financial management have become important – Touchstone was one of the early associations to be approved for derivatives trading. Our research has confirmed the significance of understanding the organisation and its needs and the proactive interaction with the environment for innovation initiation. Thus a clear understanding of issues within and without the organisation, which comes from the gestation period, helps create "a conducive organisational climate" (Van de Ven et al, 1999, p 28) for innovation.

The 'shocks' or 'triggers' that initiated innovation were associated with internal organisational issues and changes in the external environment. Internal factors included the identification of poor organisational performance, 'perceived high costs', focusing a disproportionate amount of time on a small number of tenants, and 'disappointments' with aspects of the organisation, such as feeling that the organisation was not delivering what customers wanted. One officer commented that "it is no good performing highly in an area rated less importantly by tenants while performing poorly in a highly rated area of the service". Associations also identified national and local policy arenas, for example the ways in which the introduction of private finance gave associations the freedom to pursue particular projects or the ways in which funding decisions at a local level alerted the organisation to the need for change. Similarly environmental change spurred associations to innovate, notably the growing turbulence and unanticipated policy implementation outcomes which emerged during the early years of the marketisation projects: reducing funding; the emergence of issues of poverty and deprivation; poverty traps; and so on, as discussed in Chapter 2. Internal organisational pride and the desire on the part of the executive and board members for success provided 'shocks'. This was linked to ideas associated with quality programmes at two of our case-studies: Touchstone spoke of 'wanting to be the best' while a mantra for Riverside was 'more for less' and 'better services at lower costs'.

Box 1: Triggering the 'Successful Tenancies' project at Black Country Housing Association

The project was driven by external pressures, including the changing nature of housing management. Discussion of the project began at a time when social exclusion was beginning to be widely talked about and was soon to be a major theme of the newly elected Labour government's social policies. It was also being acknowledged by housing professionals that housing management was becoming more difficult and was a task beyond core business alone; rather it was about reducing voids and turnover and managing low demand. Associations were beginning to look at ways to be more proactive in their management techniques. The Successful Tenancies project built on this background and on Black Country's role as a founder member of People for Action. This provided opportunities for information exchange and provided the trigger to undertake this project.

'Successful Tenancies' was a project aimed at 'getting it right' from the start on estates through actively encouraging tenants to participate in discussions about the development of the estate. It was allied to a similar project identifying unsuccessful estates in the Association's portfolio.

Black Country Housing Association is based in Sandwell and Dudley. It owns 1,300 properties. In recent years it has received a number of Innovation and Good Practice grants for its 'housing plus' work.

Innovation responsibility was vested in the senior executives and their relationship with the board highlights conflict and tension in this area of innovation management. Board members, however, did encourage the development of new ideas to meet housing needs through challenging the boundaries of current organisational activity but as decision makers were keen to establish the legality and risk of proposed innovations. These tensions sometimes meant that the negotiation with the board over the initiation of innovation might take many years. At East Dorset Housing Association it took some three years for the board to agree to expand the geographical area of their operations. This was because some members of the board were keen to keep their operational area to that of the former local authority and thereby retain their traditional identity. Other board members, but in particular the executive, wanted to expand their area of operation to enhance their capacity to undertake new and challenging projects. Conversely, Coventry Churches' board members, under the pre–1988 funding regime, encouraged staff to search out solutions to meet needs and would not reject any ideas without thinking them through and working out these implications for the organisation. The current financial regime and their subsequent experiences have made them a little more circumspect but left an underlying expectation from staff.

Strategies to gain board approval for resources for new projects were varied. They included citing examples of good practice elsewhere, strategic reviews of critical areas to raise the position of issues higher on the agenda or executives simply raising what were to become substantial innovations as items of any other business! Once decision makers and leaders had been exposed to an idea for an innovation they had to produce business cases to support their development. The performance targets in business plans to boards were often very high, if not unattainable, to persuade resource controllers to sponsor the project. At Riverside Housing Association a demonstration project was aimed to reduce costs, increase performance, increase customer satisfaction and improve staff morale with fewer staff. Not surprisingly it floundered, but made specific strides in management innovations and organisational efficiency, not least demonstrating the capacity for telephone-based housing management services (Walker, 1998).

The majority of the innovations required internal resources for development; thus approval from the board was the critical factor in taking their projects forward. This flexibility was welcomed by the associations and contrasted to the pre-1988 regime which did not give them the resources to undertake their own projects so easily. In nearly all our cases consultants were used. East Dorset used consultants as a form of 'organisational slack', a clear innovation management technique open to smaller organisations to boost their innovative capacity and raise their profile against the innovative association. They could develop new ideas or projects and help to achieve organisational legitimacy for them. They therefore brought expert knowledge, and were able to adapt it to the needs of the association, 'reinventing' ideas and helping to develop new ways of working.

The capacity to challenge, experiment and initiate innovation is clearly contingent upon an association's history. The innovative schemes for older people developed by Touchstone Housing Association during the 1980s were associated with the chief executive's private sector background, a 'go-ahead' management style and the use of a new product-development team (Thomas, 1987). This helped establish an innovative culture at the apex of the organisation, where key players remain, and led to ongoing stories of innovative endeavours. The chief executive of Riverside believed that "you need to take the next leap forward before you have got to the top of the last one [new initiative]". By contrast East Dorset did not have the same history. Its major innovation was the transfer, and as one of the early innovators in this field it took the association a number of years to adapt to the new environment, having few peers to learn from or benchmark themselves against.

Innovations advanced by 'entrepreneurs' following their reading of triggers or shocks could often appear to be idiosyncratic visions or projects. Comments such as: "you can't provide housing services down the telephone", in relation to the development of call centres, or about ideas just not being in tune with current thinking were often heard. However, the resource controllers and wider organisational members did not often have the full set of information to understand and comprehend the innovation in question. Indeed, the innovation idea might not have been clearly fleshed out at the time the support was being sought from resource controllers – the development of innovations dealt with this issue.

Box 2: Securing support and resources for the Gold Service Scheme, Irwell Valley Housing Association

The project secured high-level support from the chief executive, from senior politicians and housing figures, including the Prime Minister Tony Blair and the Minister for Housing, Hilary Armstrong MP, following the exposure of the idea in the media. There was some concern within the organisation that exposing the idea for the Gold Service Scheme at an early stage was a risk because the project was only at the ideas stage, lacking flesh on the bones. The idea had to be developed quickly as a result of the support gathered. With hindsight this is seen as a benefit and prompted Irwell Valley to develop the idea into a workable project.

Irwell Valley was committed to undertake the Gold Service using their own resources, and additional support from the Housing Corporation's Innovation and Good Practice (IGP) grant came after the high-level support had been obtained. However, the Housing Corporation had been by-passed until this stage, and was only made aware of the project by the Housing Minister and critical comments on the idea in the housing press. There is a feeling within the organisation that the Housing Corporation wanted the Association to have an IGP grant as a means of retaining some control over the Gold Service concept. The IGP funding allowed the project to develop some elements that would not otherwise have been possible. One welcomed outcome of the Corporation's involvement was its insistence upon the formation of an independent monitoring panel. This meets on a 6-8-week basis to discuss and evaluate the scheme. Its membership is broad, including notable figures such as Julian Richer, owner of *Richer Sounds* chain of hi-fi stores. Richer approached Irwell Valley to become involved after reading an article about Tom Manion in the *Mail on Sunday*. He has since become chair of the monitoring panel and his involvement has been important in taking the project forward. One area in which this has been seen is the availability of senior staff from Richer's companies to provide consultancy support to Irwell Valley.

Gold Service is an incentive scheme, similar to supermarket loyalty schemes, which aims to promote a culture of prompt payment and good behaviour by rewarding tenants who stick to their tenancy agreement.

Irwell Valley Housing Association is a local housing association in Manchester. It manages over 4,500 homes in the eight local authority areas of Greater Manchester. The Association has recently undergone a considerable cultural change programme following a change in chief executive.

Developing innovation

The development of innovation was a complex process. The proliferation of our studied innovations, that is the way an innovation developed from a simple idea into a number of innovations, varied by classification (Chapter 4). For example, total high-risk innovations tended to be particularly likely to proliferate. This was a product of the process of transferring visions and ideas into concrete products and processes. Innovations involving user discontinuity also had a high level of proliferation. The development of a housing-plus approach resulted in extensive proliferation as partners and customers identified a range of new services and products that could be delivered once the initial ideas and projects had been fleshed out and developed within the organisation. Organisational expansion innovations were also highly fluid, new opportunities being created or presented as organisations searched for new funding sources or operating markets. Associations often ran with a number of new products: for example Touchstone was simultaneously exploring private renting, non-traditional house-building techniques, partnering, and so on. This spread risk and reduced the possibility of innovation termination within one part of the organisation and the need to start a new innovation process on the back of a recent failure. This meant that there were other projects to focus on and the hopes of innovation team members were not as seriously damaged. Thus there were 'families' of innovations. Some of the small-scale developmental innovations examined did not, however, proliferate. These were often changes to policy and procedure and were instigated by failing processes, for example staff not using processes or they had become dated, and involved the re-specification and development of the process and training to gain staff support to adopt and use the procedure.

A number of blocks to innovation existed, which could lead to setbacks. These were often a product of the changing environment, and plans that were not properly calibrated. All our case-study associations identified regulation as restricting and slowing down innovation because it is a bureaucratic process that places too strong an emphasis upon organisational control. In particular the movement into economic regulation, through the control or rents, was argued to impact negatively upon our case-study associations and affected their ability to put in place planned innovations and service improvements. This is an example of an externally imposed innovation impacting upon organisations in unanticipated ways. The regulatory regime was viewed as increasingly prescriptive, and could have longer-term viability and flexibility impacts that would hamper innovation capacity, particularly the proposals on rent reform (DETR, 2000).

Resources (funding and time) were seen to limit innovative capacity in a number of ways. It was felt that ideas were not always taken forward because of cost/time pressures. Innovation could in itself produce this outcome. At Riverside one factor that gave it innovative capacity was its 'organisational slack': the ability to move people and thus expertise around the organisation for innovation. However, the efficiency gains made in the organisation as a result of innovation reduced this option, leading to concerns about innovation capacity. Similarly the organisation ran into time, technology and cost problems which led to it shelving its work on document imaging, part of its call centre innovation. This innovation was later reawakened when resources permitted. Innovation could mean that staff felt overstretched and unable to reflect upon their work. Consequently, for all individuals the greatest impact was the lack of time available to think about change and innovation – ironically because they were often too busy coping with the last change to manage the current round of innovation. Poorly laid innovation plans could lead to later problems when resource controllers demanded that timetables be met. For example, projects had to go live without the necessary testing being undertaken and customers therefore experiencing excessive teething problems, or resources might not be available for subsequent activities such as training which might be used to sustain innovation implementation.

> **Box 3: Changing performance and success criteria in the Amphion project (Amicus, Hastoe and Hyde Housing Associations)**
>
> The project's success (promoting new methods of sustainable construction) is assessed against the 'Egan' (1988) report. These criteria have remained fairly static throughout the project and it is realised by all involved that it is a long-term project. To assess overall success or failure would be unproductive. However, the timescales envisaged by

the consortium partners at the outset of the project have changed. Targets have not been met for a variety of reasons, and in particular the partnering agreement took more time to secure than it was thought. Furthermore, there is a recognition that cost savings have not been realised in a short timescale and that these will only emerge over time. This has prompted the associations to seek continued support and commitment, in terms of the volume of output, from the government as a means of underpinning the project.

The time factor was partly a result of the increasing size of the project – it is now seen as inevitable that reaching agreement among 20 partners would take time.

Amphion is a response by the housing association sector to the challenges of the Egan report and is aimed at improving the technology of housebuilding construction through the use of new techniques.

Amphion is a consortium led by three housing associations. Hyde Housing Association manages 25,000 properties in London and the South East with 4,000 in the development pipeline. Amicus is the parent for three associations, including Swale, an initiator of Amphion. Swale manages 11,000 homes in South London and Kent. Hastoe, the third partner, manages 2,500 properties across the South of England and focuses on environmental issues.

Innovation team members were a mixture of staff appointed to the project, seconded full-time or part-time staff with other responsibilities. They were chosen to ensure that a range of skills, competencies and attributes were available to develop the innovation. The use of staff fully dedicated to the development of the innovation ensured that continuity problems did not occur and that vital information was not lost. Many of the staff researched were also learning about innovation on the job, having never been members of a 'new product development team' before. Fluidity in personnel occurred in some situations. For example, Touchstone, in its use of BPR (business-process re-engineering), created innovation teams for each new project. It also separated the development of ideas from the piloting and implementation of innovations, thus introducing new people into the innovation processes at key stages and gaining new perspectives and appropriate competencies. Teams were encouraged and supported by top management who played a number of roles in the innovation process. The role of top management was important in ensuring successful implementation. Examples of top management interest waning resulted in the termination of projects. Top managers could also bring excessive uncertainty to the innovation process by not clarifying reporting lines and hierarchical relationships, and in a few cases have been a block to innovation. This resulted in an unfocused innovation effort and task duplication that could be particularly problematic when resource controllers had laid down limited timescales.

Box 4: The role of managers in gaining staff support for innovation, Business-Process Re-engineering at Thames Valley Housing Association

Gaining the support of staff was anticipated to be the major issue prior to the start of the project. As a result there was a conscious decision made to spend time getting staff on board. Staff were involved in the process in the stages following the tenant survey. With tenants' views of the service and what is valued, a rough vision was developed. Staff were heavily involved in redesigning the 'processes' of delivering the service.

One of the key aims of the project was not to increase staffing. There appeared to be some concern among staff that this was shorthand for staff cuts. Therefore much of the early resistance was overcome by reassuring staff that there would be no redundancies.

The project team are aware that there were periods of resistance. The resistance described was not persistent nor was it a block to change in the organisation – staff had many questions which appeared to higher-level management to be quite low level. Consequently resistance was overcome through the use of open house sessions where concerns and queries could be openly raised. Answering these queries was an essential and important element to the development of the project. In many ways it was a means of providing the staff with both clarity of what was going on and a sense of ownership of the project. Furthermore, the benefits were sold to staff in terms of their own career development and increased, up-to-date skills in addition to the benefits that the organisation would gain.

It was seen as inevitable that there would be pockets of harder-core resistance in the organisation. However, the project team seemed surprised at the low number involved in this. Indeed, those who were against the project most often left Thames Valley.

Support was enhanced through the changes made to the staffing structure. All staff had to reapply for new positions based around the structures that emerged from BPR, notably the service centre. In all it was suggested that only one member of staff was redeployed to a position because of unsuitability to the new structure. A handful of staff did not get positions that they wanted but appear to have settled into their new roles.

Thames Valley Housing Association is a medium-sized housing association, managing approximately 3,500 rented and 2,500 shared ownership homes in the South East. Thames Valley is committed to new working practices, expanding its business and offering greater customer service.

Box 5: The role of managers: a case of limited support for a community initiative

The idea for a community project was identified by an officer who researched the demands of tenants for a range of services (including gardening). Having established the demand for these services, the officer then wrote a business plan outlining the nature and extent of the demands for the service, and how unemployed local people could be trained and employed to provide these services.

The project was considered to be risky, and was left with the officer (and later a project manager) by the line manager, who indicated that as it was a risky project she did not wish to give time or support to it. The line manager has been described as a block to the innovation, through being too slow in giving support to various stages of the innovation, and even putting obstacles in the way of the innovation, through refusing to be flexible on key issues.

The project has since become successful, and has won many awards. The line manager is now showing interest in the innovation, and is trying to block the next phase because the aim of the project is to lead from within the community rather than from within the association. The relationship has become significantly strained for a mediator between the project team and the line manager to be required.

Managers at many levels in the organisation were involved in managing the development of innovations. At lower levels, the project group managers were seen to be restructuring the organisation in anticipation of the implementation of innovations. At Riverside restructuring was ongoing in the organisation's operational divisions in anticipation of the diffusion of its call centre. Restructuring could also be into temporary 'product development teams' as discussed above or permanent teams that were seen in examples of organisational expansion (marketing teams) and housing plus (community development teams). These were created to capture and focus newly identified key competencies. However, some new, specially created permanent teams often were not well integrated, were bolted on to existing activities, or were susceptible to organisational politics and were traded between departments to retain key personnel.

Partners and partnerships played varying roles in the innovation process. Innovations were often put in place to enhance the quality of services to customers, or indeed to retain custom as the demand for social housing declined. However, the focus was on gathering information from customers through, for example, surveys or communicating change. Where tenant participation structures were in place they were often symbolic, meeting the needs of the regulator. There were examples where agendas moved so fast that issues disappeared for tenants who met relatively infrequently and were trying to remain abreast of debates. At one of the two associations with tenants on the board, senior executives felt that they were a conservative block on innovation, while at the other the tenant leaders had developed a style and rhetoric not dissimilar to the chief executive! For some tenants their contact with their association was limited to service delivery issues, and they could be unaware of major developments such as the establishment of a call centre, though they had used its services.

Partnership was very important for East Dorset which engaged with change on an ongoing basis, primarily focusing on incremental innovation following its radical innovation, transferring into a housing association in 1990. In the majority of cases it took a planned approach, investigating options and reducing risks and because it adopted incremental innovations it was able to move quickly from ideas to implementation. East Dorset sought wider support for its activities from outside agencies to enhance capacity and resources and to spread risk. More broadly, partnership could lead to unanticipated outcomes. Organisations could clash over project aims and implementation strategies could change and were seen to gain uncertainty in partnerships. Partners could also be potential competitor organisations so protocols and working practices had to be established. Partnerships were seen to bring benefits by extending competencies, resources and skills but could slow the innovation process down.

Box 6: Leading innovation, building relationships and developing partnerships in Irwell Valley's Gold Service

A range of partnerships has been formed in the development of Gold Service. Some of these partnerships are formal while in several cases more informal partnerships and cooperation have been developed. Most of the partnerships formed have been with the private sector, perhaps indicating a shift in culture within the organisation and the new direction in which this innovation is taking a public sector housing organisation.

The most notable partnership that has been developed is that with Andrew Grey of Rodney Dykes Consultants. While his involvement became a stipulation of the Housing Corporation following the Innovation and Good Practice grant, he was involved at an early stage in the development of the ideas of the project. In some ways he could be seen as a poacher turned gamekeeper. Yet the consultant's relationship with Irwell Valley has remained positive and led to a strong development of the idea. The strength of the partnership can be seen in their incorporation in Gold Service Consulting, a joint venture between Rodney Dykes Consultants and Irwell Valley to assist other housing associations to improve their customer service.

Other associations have been involved in the project. Irwell Valley was part of a network involving four other associations in the North West who have been a benchmark for measuring the effects of the project. The other associations are learning from Irwell Valley and additional support is being sought from the Corporation to extend the project.

The formal 'partnerships' have been formed with local companies based around the bonus part of the scheme. Thus high street stores accept *Bonus Bonds* which are paid to Gold Service members. Irwell has developed a partnership with the distributor of *Bonus Bonds* that has enabled them to gain economies of scale when taking the concept to other areas. However, the less visible informal partnerships are arguably most important. These have involved information exchange between the Association and a number of private sector companies. Staff at the Association have attended marketing courses, also attended by supermarket chains, and so on. Private sector companies were surprised to see a housing association at these events. However, due to the differentiation between the sectors, private sector companies such as Tesco did not see Irwell Valley as a competitor. The upshot of this was Irwell Valley gained access to confidential information which supermarket chains would not wish their competitors to see. Such information has been useful in developing the bonus elements of Gold Service.

Irwell Valley Housing Association is a local housing association in Manchester. It manages over 4,500 homes in the eight local authority areas of Greater Manchester. The Association has recently undergone a considerable culture change programme following a change in chief executive.

In addition to working with partners to develop specific innovations associations also worked to create the supportive infrastructure that would permit their innovations to be accepted. This could involve internal actors, gaining their support, but more often focused on major partners: the industry regulator, lenders, and local authority partners. Associations spent time 'managing' the regulator to keep it abreast of their ideas and developments to ensure that they were accepted. The regulator uses its Innovation and Good Practice grants (IGP) here both to promote and capture innovation, disseminating new ideas and approaches, and to draw innovations into its regulatory framework. Some of our stage-two associations spoke of being persuaded to have an innovation project, and felt that this was pressed upon them so that they could be monitored and observed as they developed their sometimes radical projects. The monitoring of the IGP grants, involving regular reviews, was also identified as being a hindrance to the innovation given the time needed to complete the audit.

Implementing innovation

Innovation implementation, linking old and new practices and gaining employee commitment to and appropriate use of innovation, was achieved through a mixture of mechanisms of which teamwork and performance and appraisal systems were an important element. Reinvention can be ongoing during this period as the innovation is diffused across the organisation, which in turn adapts and changes the innovation to suit its needs and situation. This is particularly so in larger, multi-site or multigroup organisations.

The housing associations studied mainly adopted a 'depth' approach to implementation particularly for the larger innovations, running pilots and demonstrations with teams of staff to understand how their innovations would perform in practice and to iron out quirks prior to diffusion across the organisation (Lindquist and Mauriel, 1989). These teams then extended the development phase, making innovations concrete while bringing about convergence between old and new practices. Three processes were identified in our case-studies:

- The importance of securing the support of a wide number of organisational members in innovation development to enhance implementation success was revealed. The membership of project management groups included sceptical board members and staff who could be 'converted to the cause' in turn to champion the innovation across the organisation.
- Because the majority of innovations were adopted innovations, the development phase involved the process of adaptation for implementation and subsequent diffusion across the organisation. The adoption process was achieved by experiments within the organisation to flesh out ideas or selectively to implement innovation (see Walker, 1998, for a detailed case-study discussion). Touchstone undertook implementation through 'pseudo-scientific' experiments with control and implementation groups to understand the innovation in practice, to attempt to control for differences between the two sites, iron out potential difficulties and link new innovation ways of working with existing organisational practices.
- Adoption and innovation reinvention was also aided by teamwork to modify the innovation to the organisation's needs. Touchstone, in addition to using teamwork in implementation, developed innovation through business-process re-engineering techniques with staff drawn from different departments with different skills across the organisation, which again helped to spread the word and secure broader organisational support for innovation.

These interdisciplinary teams, used in all our cases, worked to reduce problems in innovation implementation because they were able to highlight issues and difficulties that helped innovations to cross organisational boundaries. These techniques of 'deep' development and implementation were seen to extend knowledge about the existence of innovations across the organisation and allow for diffusion to run a smoother path. The use of teams and experiments also assisted innovation champions slowly to let go of their projects that were modified in the experimental phase and thus aided subsequent diffusion across the organisation.

A breadth strategy, where the innovation is implemented across the entire organisation simultaneously, without any period of reflection, was a less common approach. It was seen at Riverside in the early 1990s when it took some radical steps forward. Its empowerment strategy was rolled out, literally, overnight. This created some difficulties. Front-line staff asked what they were empowered to do. However, it left a legacy of flexibility and a culture of decision making at the lowest possible level. Though the full concept of empowerment was not implemented, key concepts were taken on board by staff in the organisation.

Securing wider employee commitment to innovation and seeking to ensure its appropriate use in the implementation process were both achieved through a range of performance and reward systems. Securing employee commitment was achieved by way of the developmental innovations identified in Figure 3 in particular; the cultural change programmes at our case-study associations, and more widely across the sector, also played an important role. For example, staff at Touchstone would turn to a flip chart and brainstorm as soon as a problem was identified; this activity stemmed from their Total Quality Management programmes. All three organisations spoke of empowerment as a means to promote innovation among staff to ensure that decisions were taken at the closest point to the customer. However, empowerment created tensions, particularly with front-line staff who were unsure of their boundaries of action. East Dorset's approach to empowerment again created uncertainty. Notwithstanding this it produced a climate where people were willing to 'have a go at things' and thus helped people to understand and embrace change. Front-line staff felt that the organisation was receptive to new ideas from them, seeing their ideas adopted, and that there was an opportunity for them to get involved in developments in the organisation.

Managers, both senior and intermediate, kept an overview of short- and long-term implementation issues through training. Touchstone used training to ensure that its innovations, developed through the business-process re-engineering process, were successfully implemented. Training was also given a new emphasis in the call centres because they were introducing new ways of working and had to remain abreast of developments in organisational policy in different parts of the organisation to continue to provide responsive services. As the call centres became more established they in turn were able to offer suggestions for training and new ways of working for the parts of the organisation they served. They are able to observe practices in different locations and make judgements about what works and suggest this as best practice within the organisation.

Box 7: Measuring success and failure at Black Country's social audit

Social audit is seen as an evolutionary process. Consequently success and failure are not judged by a simple yes or no. The project has succeeded in getting the association to look at itself in a new way. It has become more customer-focused: in particular it is now keen to ensure that its objectives are what its customers want. Black Country has also developed an 'evolutionary ethic', seeing problems ironed out through the refinement of the social audit technique, developing more sophisticated objectives for the organisation and new ways of measuring effectiveness.

In addition to training, a number of planned approaches were used to ensure that employees' behaviour altered and innovations were used appropriately. Individual performance measurement regimes and appraisal systems were in place at each association. These were mainly used to ensure that improved performance was achieved but also related to organisational goals, which could include innovation. For example, the performance-related pay system at Riverside was organised around operational teams, rather than individuals. This served to alter staff behaviour towards executives' goals. One target was innovation. Though the association faced a number of difficulties in operationalising the concept, it served to remind staff of what was important. Innovation has now been given its own status through the Chief Executive's Award which is given for the best innovation in the organisation. In addition to performance targets, service standards were developed in all cases and responsiveness and quality of service to tenants was stressed. Some innovations were planned to create additional capacity. For example, the call centres were designed to free up officers' time to focus on their strengths, for example technical staff on planned maintenance. These improved services to tenants were seen to demonstrate the value of innovating.

The emphasis upon the evaluation of innovation varied. Where innovation had been introduced through pilots there was an emphasis on learning and evaluation that meant that project staff felt able to contribute towards its implementation and longer-term sustainability. However, front-line staff often felt that projects or innovations were neither fully evaluated nor lessons learnt from them, particularly if executive leadership moved on to another project. At the corporate level clear lessons were learnt about issues such as the role of project management in innovation implementation. Innovations themselves could have unanticipated outcomes. At Riverside communication became problematic or even 'anti-innovation' because the divisionalisation and the performance-related pay projects clashed. The operational units (divisions) which once worked together and shared information were put in competition with each other, creating internal barriers to communication. This has been addressed by the introduction of regular meetings between managers from the different divisions and the removal of innovation from the performance-related pay systems.

An overview of the innovation process: Riverside's Customer Service Centre

Figure 4 provides an illustrative process diagram of the way that innovation is managed. The case is the development of the Customer Service Centre at Riverside.

A number of triggers inside and outside the association were registering in the mid-1990s that were a force for a major review of service provision and organisational structure. These were explored in a demonstration project entitled STAMP (South Team Area Management Patch) which operated in 5% of their stock. This sought to redefine service delivery and the organisation of housing management and maintenance services. The STAMP project suffered a number of early setbacks, notably when the project champion moved on to another organisation. However, the success of telephone-based working – the STAMP project office was some six miles from the homes it managed – led senior managers to develop proposals and then a project team for a call centre. The call centre was project managed by a group that included senior executives, board members and project officers. This group remained in place until the call centre was implemented across the organisation. Consultants who brought technical call centre knowledge and skills in project management aided the group. The development of

Figure 4: A stylised innovation process for the Customer Service Centre (CSC) at Riverside Housing Association

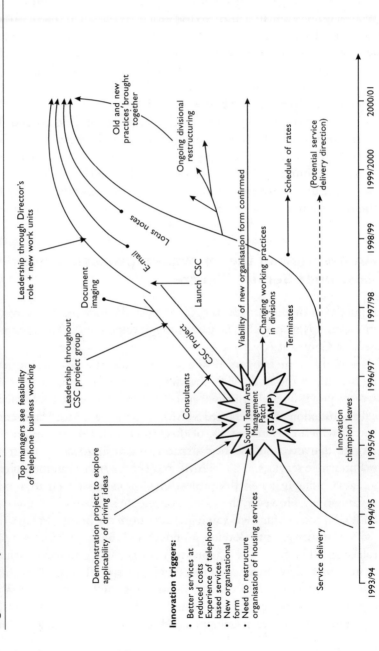

e-mail and Intranet software has helped to transform the organisation, and not just service delivery functions connected to the call centre. The Association had the technology to develop e-mail some five year earlier but needed this project to bring this innovation back to life. However, a number of setbacks have occurred. In particular the Association has faced difficulties implementing document imaging and has terminated and recommenced this project on a number of occasions due to resource and technical problems. Such a major innovation as a call centre has led to ongoing restructuring across the Association in anticipation of and because of the call centre. Pilot call centres were established in divisions to anticipate the call centre's arrival and to develop some local knowledge about it. It has also given managers the opportunity to restructure work teams to deal with particular issues, such as repairs problems, arrears or areas of low demand. The initial scepticism of staff has ebbed, though the call centre is still sometimes seen to produce problems, and old ways of working are gradually being replaced as new meets old.

Discussion

The way the housing associations in our study have adopted and implemented their innovations vary. However, there are common techniques and approaches. The techniques of teams, experiments, demonstrations and project groups have been used to help people understand and implement innovations. They have also allowed skills to be combined as and when needed. The reliance on a depth approach to the management of innovation has ensured that top-level managers are seen to retain an interest in experiments or demonstration projects, and do not create projects which are easily open to attack and criticism. In addition to the important role of top management, powerful innovation champions and process sponsors are necessary, especially when setbacks occur (Van de Ven et al, 1999). Disruptions and delays are inevitable in the innovation journey and it is important to pre-programme key events, or staging posts, to work to – conferences, peak times, and so on – to ensure that anticipated and unanticipated events can be accommodated. Finally there needs to be flexibility about the implementation of innovation; senior managers may hold a very different view from front-line staff, and these tensions need careful management.

SEVEN

Conclusions

It has been demonstrated that housing associations have innovative capacity – a sizeable proportion have lived up to the expectations placed upon them. They have steered their way through a difficult and turbulent environment and now, more than any time previously, need to maintain this capacity and enhance their ability for framebreaking. This is necessary because government agendas are now fast-moving while the expectations of the public are changing: no longer do tenants flock to the doors of the housing office in search of accommodation; the housing officer now needs to search for new tenants. The drivers of innovation now extend beyond government expectations, which has created a climate for public services organisations to present themselves as innovative organisations, and increasingly include market pressures as users exercise choice and private financiers leave their mark. They also extend to the changing nature of the external environment and the ways in which our case-study associations actively engaged with it. In addition leaders were eager to improve performance across a number of dimensions and keen to learn from other contexts. The iterative process of innovation and re-regulation of these new activities by associations, to draw them into a framework where they can be monitored, is clearly seen in our example of housing associations. Associations have responded to changes in their environment and developed a range of innovations which has led the industry regulator to redesign the regulatory framework. It can be argued that this has been designed in such a way that it can bend and flex, going with the flow of the innovations that associations put into practice, rather than snap and shatter as the flow of innovations is resisted. However, in order to achieve this, the control over associations has been increased raising a challenge to future housing association innovation. The style of regulation now seen is more akin to that of the privatised utilities, with a growing emphasis upon economic regulation. This in part reflects the housing associations' own self-definitions, and their capacity for polymorphism; they increasingly parade themselves as private organisations, but can still display their public and voluntary forms. This final chapter of our study draws out conclusions and makes linkages between the central questions of this book concerning the classification of innovation, the characteristics of innovative organisations and the management of innovation.

The nature of housing association innovations

As change and turbulence in the environment becomes endemic, innovation has been presented as the antidote, offering confidence and a new lease of life; associations will have the capacity to go on to meet the next phase of uncertainty that they will face. While it was implicitly assumed that this form of independent non-profit organisation was innovative and able to meet new challenges, no evidence had been previously presented to support this case. The evidence presented in this book now indicates that housing associations do have innovative capacity – they are capable of framebreaking activities rather than just framebending. Just under 20% of 'active' associations were drawn into our database, and a similar proportion of total innovations identified in comparison to the private sector studies. We have developed a two-stage innovation classification system to describe these innovations. This allows broader generalisations to be made from the findings and provides information for practitioners about the management implications of the innovations they are adopting. The innovations developed by associations have been summarised under the headings of:

- diversification,
- organisational expansion,
- customer focus,
- organisation structures, and
- new management techniques.

These innovations have been classified and given primary attributes:

- total innovation: providing new services to new users,
- evolutionary innovation: providing new services to existing customers,
- expansionary innovation: providing existing services to new users, and
- developmental or incremental innovations: modifying services and provision which have supported the range of total, expansionary and evolutionary innovations.

These innovations have also been shown to have additional characteristics. The second stage of our classification system highlighted the importance of organisational focus, radicalness, centrality, adaptability, uncertainty, pervasiveness and risk. Thus total innovations can vary, requiring different skills, commitments and innovation management.

The innovative housing association

Our research has demonstrated that innovation is more likely to be found in some associations than in others. The 'typical' innovative housing association, based upon our literature-derived database at the end of the 1990s, has the following characteristics:

- it will be a larger association with 6,000 homes, if not more;
- it will have specialist staff, with support and development staff being particularly important, whereas a large number of housing management staff will reduce the capacity for innovation;
- it will have a high proportion of professional staff;
- it will work in nearly thirty different local authorities, if not more;
- it will have a variety of tasks and functions bringing together different skills and departments.

The innovative housing association fits the picture of a 'regional' association. This is a significant finding given the likely transfer of swathes of local government housing stock into the association sector over the next decade – anticipated to be at the rate of 200,000 units a year. The government has suggested that the maximum size of a transfer association should be 12,000 homes. This ceiling, which many organisations are likely to approach, would suggest that the innovation will continue apace in the sector because of the significance accorded to size in our analysis. However, transfer organisations are unlikely to score on the range of variables that characterise the innovative association. For example, they will be geographically restricted, initially, to one locality, or part thereof, and have limited functional differentiation (for example only one or two departments such as general needs and sheltered housing). Furthermore, the process of adaptation and change following transfer was a long and slow one in our example. We could therefore see innovation decrease in proportionate and absolute terms, as the nature of the sector is transformed.

Our findings indicate the significance of other factors. We have highlighted the development team. However, given the changing nature of the development process, which has moved away from greenfield new build to regeneration, it is possible to hypothesise that substantial regeneration activity, which would include housing plus, at an association could bring the same dynamic process. However, the critical difference here is the expansionary activities that a development team have over a regeneration team. Thus an organisation that is increasing in size is important, and, as was discussed in Chapter 5, size in itself is important.

These findings lead to the conclusion that the innovative association might not fit the ideal type of organisation that is alluded to in government publications. It might be neither regeneration- and tenant-focused nor specialise in the delivery of housing management services in the context of social exclusion but more managerial in its composition. Evidence presented from other research (Clapham, 1992) indicates that small organisations, with less than 1,000 homes, are more conducive to good organisational performance and high levels of tenant involvement. However, such organisations do not necessarily have the capacity to influence the institutional bodies of housing policy (Clapham and Kintrea, 2000). This suggests that the policy objectives laid down by government may be mutually incompatible: innovation equals big, tenant-friendly equals small. Given that many pressures are towards larger organisations we conclude that associations will continue to innovate.

Managing innovation in housing associations

In concluding that innovations will continue to be developed in the housing association sector, though perhaps at a slower pace than in the recent past due to the large transfer programme, recommendations on the management of innovation are more pressing. Based upon our theoretical framework and the evidence collected in the case-studies, public services organisations should not expect innovation to be a smooth journey of regular staging posts and clear signposts signalling the next step on the journey. Rather, innovation is a journey through uncharted waters that will lead organisations down stray tributaries that become un-navigable and through the rush of rapids that leads the initiation, development and implementation of innovation. The clear lessons on the management of innovation to emerge from this study are:

- Boundary-scanning activities provide an important store of knowledge that aids future innovation initiation and development by looking outside the sector and bringing ideas back to it.
- Leaders need to be willing to challenge the status quo and consider new ways of doing things to be ahead of the game.
- Innovation capacity is greater where associations proactively interact with their environment as well as understanding their own needs. However, looking outside is not the function of leaders alone.
- The process of securing resources for innovation projects often leads the innovation champion to overstate the likely performance achievements of the project to gain support.
- Innovations will proliferate into various projects as they are developed. This is to be expected as ideas flow from the original concept. Bundles or families of innovations are useful ways to ensure that a final innovation is delivered as setbacks frequently occur on the innovation journey. Alternative and complementary innovations are one way to ensure forward movement in the search for continuous improvement.
- Interdisciplinary project teams are essential for successful innovation development and implementation. They allow a range of skills, competencies and attitudes to be brought together to match the need of the project. Teams also facilitate innovation implementation by 'spreading the word' and demonstrating how the new and old can be combined to move forward.
- Experiments, demonstration projects and selective implementation were used to flesh out innovation ideas and work up projects into clear policies and procedures for implementation across the wider organisation, providing the innovation team and others within the association with evidence of what works. This 'deep' development and implementation of innovation resulted in the successful diffusion of innovations within the associations, but is contingent upon top management's continued sponsorship and championing of innovation projects. It also allowed others to anticipate the arrival of new ways of working and explore, within their own setting, the likely impact of the innovation.
- Partnership innovations will be more complex to manage than internal innovations and associations should expect more setbacks and a higher level of conflict while changing personnel can elongate project timescales.
- Full implementation of innovations will be enhanced by management practices that reinforce the desired innovation behaviour in staff. Performance systems that identified clearly to staff the desired

behaviour were successful in achieving this, whether they were directly linked to pay or to appraisal systems. These help to overcome the difficult process of unlearning old practices and bringing about new ways of behaving.

The impact of innovation has been substantial on our case-study organisations, leading to discontinuity and suggesting that innovation is a cyclical process bringing back new and old issues in unforeseen ways. As well as newly placing emphasis upon teams, project management and product development teams, associations are now engaged in developing new skills. These include marketing skills for a new group of users in the private rented sector or people and community management skills for housing plus. Some housing associations had previously developed these skills in the 1970s as associations worked on a range of renewal projects. However, and has been noted elsewhere (Greer and Hoggett, 1999), strategic skills have become important for housing associations as the policy role has increasingly been taken by government and the funder–regulator and organisations focus upon their niche and strategic position.

One of the most significant impacts of innovation has been to reinforce the longstanding tension between property and people approaches in the housing management service. This broader example, with evidence drawn from our cases, clearly highlights the cyclical nature of innovation. Housing management has moved between an emphasis upon property and people at various points throughout its history. The new financial regime for associations brought core business to prominence and promoted a performance culture (Walker, 1994; Walker and Smith, 1999). This took them away from the regeneration and renewal work that typified the endeavours of many associations in the 1970s. The pendulum swung during the 1990s and vastly reduced the welfare aspects of housing management work. This occurred at the same time as the welfare problems of tenants increased. Walker (2000) has noted how innovation tensions such as these are magnified by innovations such as call centres, and particularly between traditionally trained staff and new entrants to the sector. The former emphasise the altruistic aspects of housing management work and the latter efficiency and more generic customer care. The concentration of a wide range of service delivery functions into one specially created organisational unit, a call centre, which is more mechanistic than the rest of the organisation, has led to far-reaching ramifications for staff and the organisation of work. One facet of this has been a return to specialisation in housing management work. This breaks from generic patches where housing officers were responsible for all aspects of housing management and 'knew' their tenants. Though benefits are seen to come from specialisation in terms of higher performance and the ability to focus on wider strategic issues, including the needs of tenants, officers still highlighted the loss of personal contact. These tensions will only continue as associations increase their innovation efforts, managing innovation as an ongoing venture in their newly diversified and complex organisations.

Tracking housing association innovation for best practice

The findings reported in this study have been supported by a longitudinal methodology. In the current climate of 'evidence-based policy and practice' such approaches ensure evidence emerges and not snapshots of organisations who rationalise and present their 'best side' to the researcher who parachutes in for a day or two. This needs to be juxtaposed with the more normative climate surrounding innovation since the election of the Labour government, and the concomitant increase in claims of innovation resulting from schemes such as 'beacon' status in local government. Nonetheless two of our research approaches are worthy of additional discussion.

First, we have researched the management of innovation through time adopting the longitudinal, contextual and comparative case-study methodology from the change research literature (Pettigrew et al, 1988). This approach has allowed us to draw practical conclusions on the management of innovation reported above. We have been able to provide findings about the 'what' of innovation and classify housing associations' activities; issues surrounding 'why' innovations are developed have been explained; and 'how' innovation is managed in housing associations has been explored. Such techniques could be usefully adapted across the housing association sector and other public services to explore questions of innovation or broader concerns with organisational effectiveness.

Second, we have also provided the first baseline of innovative activity in the housing association sector through our adoption of the Literature-Based Innovation Output Indicator (LBIOI) in the public services sector. This has shown that associations have primarily developed innovations to their existing customers and incremental innovations, with examples of total and expansionary innovations. Databases such as this provide government and its agencies with the opportunity to establish longitudinal studies that will mean that:

- innovation can be tracked over time to understand the nature of the innovations being developed;
- the changing innovativeness of a sector can be monitored and compared with other public services sectors;
- the relationship between innovation and performance can be explored to develop cutting-edge best practice.

What is more is that these techniques can be developed without burdening organisations through questionnaire surveys, because they rely upon bibliographic techniques, and are therefore easy to maintain. If housing associations were willing to provide data in a questionnaire on a regular basis these data sets could be further improved. They also allow best practice to be easily identified to public services organisations and their decision makers and make evidence widely available. We strongly urge government and its agencies to consider the adoption of these techniques in their research and support for and dissemination of innovation.

Innovation and regulation

The Blair government has provided continuity in management reforms with the previous Conservative administration of John Major by expanding the regulation of public services. The NHS has two new regulatory agencies promoting excellence and inspecting hospitals. Some local government services are now experiencing regulation as the Best Value Inspectorate extends to other parts not previously reached by existing inspection agencies. The Best Value regime can learn from the housing association sector. Best Value is a continuous improvement regime where local authority services are inspected on their processes for improvement and their performance. The housing association regime has had these characteristics for a number of years while being a sector where innovation has taken place.

We have argued that innovation and regulation are simultaneously concerned with change: innovation with discontinuous change and regulation with effecting change to achieve predetermined standards through the collection of information. Housing associations have been challenging the framework of predetermined standards set for them –

indeed housing associations have been smashing through this regulatory net. Through this study we have seen the regulator legitimating housing association innovation: housing associations have been challenging regulatory boundaries to achieve discontinuity and the Housing Corporation has brought these innovations into their net through its regulatory instruments, and revised the regulatory regime and its sponsorship of innovation.

What makes the regulation of the innovations discussed here complex is the dynamic nature of the innovation process. Therefore, it is difficult for the regulator to set standards and monitor new developments because uncertainty exists about them, standards of behaviour have not been established and no monitoring data exists to be collected on their performance. The promotion of innovation and good practice by the regulator attempts to capture this discontinuity and challenges to its framework while simultaneously indicating its expectations of associations. Standard setting and the effecting of change are therefore controlled to reflect what the regulator sees as the key issues and provides a climate for innovation within boundaries. Current attempts by the regulator (Housing Corporation, 1999) to limit the proportion of activity that is non-core or innovatory are a direct result of these difficulties. This leads to a number of scenarios.

Scenario one envisages a vast reduction in the scope and extent of the regulatory framework. The Corporation seeks to make the regulatory barrier less brittle and more pliable, so it is able to watch it bow and flex but not break. If it begins to reach what is defined as the breaking point, alarm bells should have been ringing for some time. Within these perimeters associations are free to innovate.

The second scenario suggests a problematic regime where an ever-tightening regulatory framework leads to a straitjacket which produces mechanistic structures and processes that are not conducive to innovation. A regulatory framework that permits innovation needs to be able to detect new activity but not stop associations developing new products or services. Change can then be effected if the direction of the innovation is inappropriate. However, given the new regulatory regime together with proposals for reform, notably those on rents which some associations see as being sufficiently punitive as to undermine their innovatory capacity, it is possible to suggest that the regime is becoming increasingly centralised at a time when associations are becoming more reliant upon other sources of funding besides those of the Housing Corporation. Thus the 'privately financed independent public housing organisation' will be closely watched and may find its innovation capacity restricted.

A third scenario, and the conclusions we draw based upon the findings presented here, however, is not so pessimistic. While it may remain necessary to have a strong regulatory regime to monitor and scrutinise associations, they themselves have been innovating and framebreaking for a number of years. It is likely that change to the regulatory regime to capture this activity will not stop associations innovating nor the regulator developing new innovative policies. In particular, associations have the capacity to innovate, they have ongoing problems to resolve and new market pressures to respond to, and therefore innovation will continue apace. In this scenario we can envisage the creation of a virtuous innovation loop where regulator actions and association behaviour enhance the innovative capacity of the sector and increase the nature and extent of housing association innovation. For associations the 'shocks' setting them off on the 'innovation journey' will include the changes in the external environment, including growing market pressures as discussed in Chapter 3, and the actions of the regulator. For example, movement into the area of economic regulation, responding to limited market processes in the sector, could provide innovations, given the evidence from the privatised utilities. This single innovation loop is supplemented by a further one as the innovation architecture grows, notably the innovation and good practice regime and the emerging Best Value regime.

The clear lesson to housing associations is that if they want to be innovative they need to challenge the boundaries of their activities to deliver the innovations they have been identifying over the last decade as necessary to deal with their changing external environment. This will include scanning the environment for new opportunities while understanding the attributes of innovations and the management skills needed for adoption and implementation. This relationship between the regulator and housing associations can therefore provide a framework that allows for successful innovation because associations try to break the mould while the regulator develops new proposals and policies that 'shock' associations into innovative activity. Consequently we propose that organisations will innovate in highly regulated sectors by 'challenging the boundaries' but that regulator restriction of the scope of organisational activity will eventually reduce innovation and damage the chance of achieving innovation and the Best Value management aims of continuous improvement and innovation itself.

Researching innovation

In this project we have developed existing knowledge in the fields of innovation, housing and public services management. In relation to innovation, two contributions have been made. First, innovation classification systems have been enhanced. The value of a full and clear classification of innovation attributes has been demonstrated by the adoption of a two-stage process. Osborne's typology of innovation has also been shown to be applicable in other public services sectors and we have demonstrated the value of the LBIOI for housing associations and the wider public services. The ability to generalise the results of this research has been improved by these two factors. Second, additional evidence to support innovation process theory has been provided. Though undertaken in a limited number of sites, the research has supported the notion that innovation is a dynamic, iterative and multidirectional process. These findings concur with those of King (1992) who also noted, as this study has, that smaller-scale innovations (here classified as development innovations) were more likely to develop in a linear or staged fashion through time. More substantive, or as Pelz (1983) classified them, radical innovations have developed in complex ways. This project has also indicated the significance of other aspects of the innovation process:

- that innovation initiation is dependent on an organisation's history;
- that temporal separations around development and implementation were difficult to specify; and
- that innovation development was frequently undertaken in such a way as to draw in a range of organisational members as a process of gaining wider organisational support to legitimise innovation.

Within housing studies and the housing association policy arena this project has also made substantive contributions. It is the first study of innovation in organisations within housing studies (see for example Barlow, 1999, on housing production). It has answered the rhetorical innovation questions posed by housing associations and institutions in the sector to indicate that housing associations do have innovative capacity. The project has also made an empirical contribution by classifying these innovations and has provided information on the innovation process. Contributions have also been made to public services management through the discussion of the innovation–regulation relationship (more fully discussed in Walker and Jeanes, 2001).

Finally, the work reflects broader changes within the public services sector. For example, in the English university sector reductions in government income and the introduction of performance regimes and forms of regulation have stratified the sector, rewarding certain institutions (Shattock, 1998) leading to the creation of the 'privately financed public university'. Pressures in the housing association sector are similarly leading to the creation of housing associations that are 'privately financed public housing associations'; this in turn fundamentally alters governance, management and accountability. If one is to develop the comparison further one is likely to see the creation of a super-league of associations which rely upon only government resources for a small element of their activity. These are likely to be the associations that currently fit the model of the 'innovative housing association'.

References

Abernathy, W., Clark, K. and Kantrow, A. (1983) *Industrial renaissance*, New York, NY: Basic Books.

Aitken, M. and Hage, J. (1971) 'The organic organisation and innovation', *Sociology*, vol 5, no 1, pp 63-82.

Anderson, N.R. and King, N. (1991) 'Managing innovation in organizations', *Leadership and Organizational Development Journal*, vol 12, no 1, pp 17-21.

Angle, H.L. and Van de Ven, A.H. (1989) 'Suggestions for managing the innovation journey', in A. Van de Ven, H.L. Angle and M.S. Poole (eds), *Research on the management of innovation: The Minnesota studies*, New York, NY: Harper and Row.

Ashby, J. (1997) 'The inquiry into housing association governance', in P. Malpass (ed), *Ownership, control and accountability. The new governance of housing*, Coventry: Chartered Institute of Housing.

Ashworth, R., Boyne, G.A. and Walker, R.M. (1999) 'Regulatory problems in the public sector: Theories and cases', paper given at the ESRC Seminar on New Labour and the Third Way in Public Services, University of Manchester, December.

Ashworth, R., Boyne, G.A. and Walker, R.M. (2001) 'Devolution and regulation: the political control of public bodies in Wales', in P. Chaney, T. Hall, and A. Pithouse (eds), *New governance – New democracy?*, Cardiff: University of Wales Press.

Audit Commission/Housing Corporation (1995) *Homing in on performance: Social housing performance compared*, London: Audit Commission/Housing Corporation.

Audit Commission/Housing Corporation (1996a) *Within site: Assessing value for money in housing associations' New Build programmes*, London: Audit Commission/Housing Corporation.

Audit Commission/Housing Corporation (1996b) *House styles: Performance and practice in housing management*, London: Audit Commission/Housing Corporation.

Audit Commission/Housing Corporation (1998) *To build or not to build: Assessing value for money in housing associations' rehabilitation programmes*, London: Audit Commission/Housing Corporation.

Barlow, J. (1999) 'From craft production to mass customisation. Innovation requirements for the UK housebuilding industry', *Housing Studies*, vol 14, no 1, pp 23-42.

Berry, F.S. (1994) 'Innovation in public management: the adoption of strategic planning', *Public Administration Review*, vol 54, no 4, pp 322-9.

Bigoness, W.J. and Perreault, Jr, W.D. (1981) 'A conceptual paradigm and approach for the study of innovators', *Academy of Management Journal*, vol 24, no 1, pp 68-82.

Borins, S. (2000) 'What Borders? Public management innovation in the United States and Canada', *Journal of Policy Analysis and Management*, vol 19, no 1, pp 46-74.

Boyne, G.A. (2001: forthcoming) 'Public and private management: what's the difference?', *Journal of Management Studies*.

Bozeman, B. (1987) *All organizations are public*, London: Jossey-Bass.

Bramley, G. (1993) 'The social housing quasi-market', in J. Le Grand and W. Bartlett (eds), *Quasi-markets and social policy*, Basingstoke: Macmillan.

Bright, J. (2000) '"Big bang" set to end council landlords', *Inside Housing*, 21 January, p 1.

Burns, T. and Stalker, G.M. (1962) *The management of innovation*, London: Tavistock Publications.

Cabinet Office (2000) *Modernising government*, London: Cabinet Office.

Clapham, D. (1992) 'The effectiveness of housing management', *Social Policy & Administration*, vol 26, pp 209-25.

Clapham, D. and Evans, A. (1998) *From exclusion to inclusion: Helping to create successful tenancies and communities*, London: Hastoe Housing Association.

Clapham, D. and Kintrea, K. (1987) 'Importing housing policy: housing co-operatives in Britain and Scandinavia', *Housing Studies*, vol 2, no 3, pp 157-69.

Clapham, D. and Kintrea, K. (2000) 'Community-based housing organisations and the local governance debate', *Housing Studies*, vol 15, pp 533-99.

Cole, I., Kane, S. and Robinson, D. (1999) *Changing demand, changing neighbourhoods: The response of social landlords*, London: Housing Corporation.

Cooke, M. (1999) 'HAs furious at public "Naming & Shaming"', *Housing Today*, issue 127, 1 April, p 1.

Coombs, R., Narandren, P. and Richards, A. (1996) 'A literature-based innovation output indicator', *Research Policy*, vol 25, pp 403-13.

Coopers & Lybrand (nd) *Housing management direct*, London: Coopers & Lybrand.

Cope, H. (1998) *Housing associations*, Basingstoke: Macmillan.

Cyert, R.M. and March, J.G. (1963) *A behavioral theory of the firm*, Englewood Cliffs, NJ: Prentice-Hall.

Damanpour, F. (1987) 'The adoption of technological, administrative, and ancillary innovations: impact of organizational factors', *Journal of Management*, vol 13, no 4, pp 675-88.

Damanpour, F. (1991) 'Organizational innovation: a meta analysis of effects of determinants and moderators', *Academy of Management Journal*, vol 34, pp 555-90.

Damanpour, F. and Evan, W.M. (1984) 'Organizational innovation and performance: the problem of "organisational lag"', *Administrative Science Quarterly*, vol 29, pp 392-409.

Dean, J.W. (1987) 'Building the future: the justification process of new technology', in J.M. Pennings and A. Buitendam (eds), *New technology as organizational innovation*, Cambridge, MA: Ballinger.

DETR (Department of the Environment, Transport and the Regions) (1998) *Modern local government: In touch with the people* (http://www.local-regions.detr.gov.uk/).

DETR (1999) *Projections of households in England 2021*, London: The Stationery Office.

DETR (2000) *Quality and choice: A decent home for all*, The Housing Green Paper, London: DETR.

DoE (Department of the Environment) (1996) *Projections of households in England to 2016* (http://www.housing.detr.gov.uk/research/project/index.htm).

Dow, S. (2000) 'Making all the right noises', *Housing Today*, 4 May, pp 12-13.

Downs, G.W. and Mohr, L.B. (1976) 'Conceptual issues in the study of innovation', *Administrative Science Quarterly*, vol 21, pp 700-14.

Egan, J. (1998) *Rethinking construction, The Report of the Construction Task Force to the Deputy Prime Minister on the scope for improving the quality and efficiency of UK construction*, London: The Stationery Office.

Ford, J. and Wilcox, S. (1994) *Affordable housing, low incomes and the flexible labour market*, London: National Federation of Housing Associations.

Golden, O. (1990) 'Innovation in public sector human service programs: the implications of innovation by "groping along"', *Journal of Policy Analysis and Management*, vol 9, no 2, pp 219-48.

Goodlad, R. (1993) *The enabling authority*, Coventry: Chartered Institute of Housing.

Greer, A. and Hoggett, P. (1999) 'Public policies, private strategies and local public spending bodies', *Public Administration*, vol 77, no 2, pp 235-56.

Hage, J. and Dewar, R. (1973) 'Elite values versus organizational structure in predicting innovation', *Administrative Science Quarterly*, vol 18, pp 279-90.

Harrow, L. and Willcocks, J. (1992) *Rediscovering public services management*, London: McGraw-Hill.

Hoggett, P. (1996) 'New modes of control in the public sector', *Public Administration*, vol 74, no 1, pp 9-32.

Holmans, A. (1997) *Housing demand and need in England 1991-2011*, York: Joseph Rowntree Foundation.

Hood, C., James, O., Jones, G., Scott, C. and Travers, T. (1999) *Regulation inside government: Waste-watchers, quality police, and sleaze-busters*, Oxford: Oxford University Press.

Hood, C., James, O. and Scott, C. (2000) 'Regulation of government: has it increased, is it increasing, should it be diminished?', *Public Administration*, vol 78, no 2, pp 283-304.

Hosking, D.M. and Anderson, N.R. (eds) (1992) *Organizational change and innovation: Psychological perspectives and practices in Europe*, London: Routledge.

Hosking, D.M. and Morley, I. (1991) *A social psychology of organizing*, London: Harvester Wheatsheaf.

Housing Corporation (1997) *A Housing Plus approach to achieving sustainable communities*, London: Housing Corporation.

Housing Corporation (1998a) *Tenant participation*, London: Housing Corporation.

Housing Corporation (1998b) *Performance standards*, London: Housing Corporation.

Housing Corporation (1998c) *Best Value and RSLs: A consultation paper*, London: Housing Corporation.

Housing Corporation (1999) *Regulating diversity*, London: Housing Corporation.

Institute for Public Policy Research (2000) *Housing united*, London: Institute for Public Policy Research.

Kanter, R.M. (1983) *The change masters*, New York, NY: Touchstone Books.

Kimberly, J.R. (1981) 'Managerial innovation', in P.C. Nystrom and W.H. Starbuck (eds), *Handbook of organisational design. Volume 1: Adapting organizations to their environments*, New York, NY: Oxford University Press.

Kimberly, J.R. and Evanisko, M.J. (1981) 'Organizational innovation: the influence of individual, organizational and contextual factors on hospitals' adoption of technological and administrative innovations', *Academy of Management Journal*, vol 24, pp 689-713.

King, N. (1992) 'Modelling the innovation process: an empirical comparison of approaches', *Journal of Occupational and Organizational Psychology*, vol 65, pp 89-100.

King, N. and Anderson, N.R. (1995) *Innovation and change in organizations*, London: Routledge.

Klein, K.J. and Sorra, J.S. (1996) 'The challenge of innovation implementation', *Academy of Management Review*, vol 21, no 4, pp 1055-80.

Langstaff, M. (1992) 'Housing associations: a move to centre stage', in J. Birchall (ed), *Housing policy in the 1990s*, London: Routledge.

Le Grand, J. and Bartlett, W. (1993) *Social policy and quasi markets*, Basingstoke: Macmillan.

Lindquist, K. and Mauriel, J. (1989) 'Depth and breadth in innovation implementation: The case of school-based management', in A.H. Van de Ven, H.L. Angle and M.S. Poole (eds), *Research on the management of innovation: The Minnesota studies*, New York, NY: Harper and Row.

Malpass, P. (1997) 'The discontinuous history of housing associations in England', paper given at the Housing Studies Association Conference, Cardiff, September.

Malpass, P (1999) 'Housing associations and housing policy in Britain since 1989', *Housing Studies*, vol 14, no 6, pp 881-93.

Meyer, A.D. and Goes, J.B. (1988) 'Organizational assimilation of innovations: A multilevel contextual analysis', *Academy of Management Journal*, vol 31, pp 897-923.

Mohr, L. (1987) 'Innovation theory: An assessment from the vantage point of new electronic technology in organisations', in J. Pennings and A. Buitendan (eds), *New technology as organizational innovation*, Cambridge, MA: Ballinger.

Mullins, D. (1997a) 'Changing with the times – housing association responses to a changing environment', in D. Mullins and M. Riseborough (eds), *Changing with the times: Critical interpretations of the repositioning of housing associations*, Occasional Paper 12, School of Public Policy, University of Birmingham.

Mullins, D. (1997b) 'From regulatory capture to regulated competition: an interest group analysis of the regulation of housing associations in England', *Housing Studies*, vol 12, no 3, pp 301-20.

Mullins, D. (1999) 'Managing ambiguity: merger activity in the nonprofit housing sector', *International Journal of Nonprofit and Voluntary Sector Marketing,* vol 4, no 4, pp 364-94.

Mullins, D. and Riseborough, M. (2000) *Changing with the times*, School of Public Policy, University of Birmingham.

Mullins, D., Niner, P. and Riseborough, M. (1993) 'Large-scale voluntary transfers', in P. Malpass and R. Means (eds) *Implementing housing policy*, Buckingham: Open University Press.

Mullins, D., Reid, B. and Walker, R.M. (2001: forthcoming) 'Modernisation and change in social housing: the case for an organisational perspective', *Public Administration*.

Newman, J., Raine, J. and Skelcher, C. (2000) *Innovation and Best Practice in local government: A research report*, London: DETR.

Normann, R. (1991) *Service management*, Chichester: John Wiley.

Osborne, D. and Gaebler, T. (1992) *Reinventing government*, Reading, MA: Addison-Wesley.

Osborne, S.P. (1998) *Voluntary organisations and innovation in public services*, London: Routledge.

Page, D. (1993) *Building communities*, York: Joseph Rowntree Foundation.

Pelz, D.C. (1983) 'Quantitative case histories of urban innovations: are there innovation stages?', *IEEE Transactions on Engineering Management*, vol 30, no 2, pp 60-7.

Peters, T. and Waterman, Jr, R. (1982) *In search of excellence*, New York, NY: Harper and Row.

Pettigrew, A., McKee, L. and Ferlie, E. (1988) 'Understanding change in the NHS', *Public Administration*, vol 66, pp 297-317.

Pettigrew, A., Ferlie, E. and McKee, L. (1992) *Shaping strategic change*, London: Sage Publications.

Pierce, J.L. and Delbacq, A.L. (1977) 'Organizational structure, individual attitudes, and innovation', *Academy of Management Review*, vol 2, pp 26-37.

Pollitt, C., Birchall, J. and Putman, K. (1998) *Decentralising public service management*, Basingstoke: Macmillan.

Pollitt, C. and Bouckaert, G. (2000) *Public management reform: A comparative analysis*, Oxford: Oxford University Press.

Power, M. (1998) *The audit society: The rituals of verification*, Oxford: Oxford University Press.

Quinn, R.E. (1988) *Beyond rational management*, London: Jossey-Bass.

Ramswamy, K., Thomas, A.S. and Litschert, R.J. (1994) 'Organizational performance in a regulated environment: the role of strategic orientation', *Strategic Management Journal*, vol 15, pp 63-74.

Reid, B. (1995) 'Interorganizational networks and the delivery of local housing services', *Housing Studies*, vol 10, no 2, pp 133-50.

Reid, B. (1999) 'Reframing the delivery of local housing services: networks and the new competition', in G. Stoker (ed), *The new management of British local governance*, Basingstoke: Macmillan.

Rogers, E. (1962) *Diffusion of innovations* (1st edn), New York, NY: Free Press.

Rogers, E. (1995) *Diffusion of innovations* (4th edn), New York, NY: Free Press.

Rogers, E. and Kim, J.-I. (1985) 'Diffusion of innovations in public sector organisations', in R. Merritt and A.J. Merritt (eds), *Innovation in the public sector*, Beverly Hills, CA: Sage Publications.

Schroeder. R.G., Van de Ven, A., Scudder, G.D. and Polley, D. (1989) 'The development of innovative ideas', in A. Van de Ven, H.L. Angle and M.S. Poole (eds), *Research on the management of innovation: The Minnesota studies*, New York, NY: Harper and Row.

SEU (Social Exclusion Unit) (2000) *National strategy for neighbourhood renewal: A framework for consultation*, London: Cabinet Office.

Shattock, M. (1998) 'The shape of things to come', *Guardian Higher*, 3 March 1999, pp ii-iii.

Slappendel, C. (1996) 'Perspectives on innovation in organizations', *Organization Studies*, vol 17, no 1, pp 107-29.

Stewart, J. (1996) 'Innovation in democratic practice in local government', *Policy & Politics*, vol 24, no 1, pp 29-41.

Thomas, A. (1987) *New homes for old: Re-housing elderly homeowners*, Coventry: Coventry Churches Housing Association.

Tushman, M.L. and Anderson, P. (1986) 'Technological discontinuities and organisational environments', *Administrative Science Quarterly*, vol 31, pp 439-65.

Tushman, M.L. and Nadler, D. (1996) 'Organizing for innovation', in K. Starkey (ed), *How organizations learn*, London: International Thomson Business Press.

Utterback, J.M. (1974) 'Innovation in industry and the diffusion of technology', *Science*, vol 183, pp 620-6.

Van de Ven, A., Angle, H.L. and Poole, M.S. (eds) (1989) *Research on the management of innovation: The Minnesota studies*, New York, NY: Harper and Row.

Van de Ven, A., Polley, D.E., Garud, R. and Venkataraman, S. (1999) *The innovation journey*, New York, NY: Oxford University Press.

Wagstaff, M. (1997) *The future of independent social housing*, London: Housing Corporation.

Walker, R.M. (1994) 'Putting performance measurement in context: classifying social housing organisations', *Policy & Politics*, vol 22, no 2, pp 191-202.

Walker, R.M. (1998) 'New public management and housing associations: from comfort to competition', *Policy & Politics*, vol 26, no 1, pp 71-87.

Walker, R.M. (2000) 'The changing nature of social housing management: the impact of externalisation and managerialisation', *Housing Studies*, vol 15, no 2, pp 239-57.

Walker, R.M. and Jeanes, E.L. (2001: forthcoming) 'Innovation in a regulated service: the case of English housing associations', *Public Management Review*.

Walker, R.M and Smith, R.S.G. (1999) 'Regulatory and organisational responses to restructured housing association finance in England and Wales', *Urban Studies*, vol 36, pp 737-54.

Whipp, R. and Clark, C. (1986) *Innovation and the auto industry: Product, process and work organisation*, London: Francis Pinter.

Wolfe, A. (1994) 'Organizational innovation: review, critique and suggested research directions', *Journal of Management Studies*, vol 31, no 3, pp 405-31.

Zaltman, G., Duncan, R. and Holbek, J. (1973) *Innovations and organizations*, New York, NY: John Wiley.

Index